The
Dream of
the Perfect Act

The Dream of the Perfect Act

An Inquiry into the Fate of Religion in a Secular World

RICHARD FENN

Tavistock Publications
New York and London

First published in 1987 by
Tavistock Publications
in association with Methuen, Inc.
29 West 35th Street, New York NY 10001

Published in the UK by
Tavistock Publications Ltd
11 New Fetter Lane, London EC4P 4EE

Printed at the University Press, Cambridge

Library of Congress Cataloging in Publication Data

Fenn, Richard K.
The dream of the perfect act.

Bibliography: p.
Includes index.
1. Sociology, Christian. 2. Intentionalism.
3. Perfection. 4. Liturgics.
5. Rites and ceremonies.
I. Title.
BT738.F44 1987   261.1   86–30025

ISBN 0–422–61300–2

British Library Cataloguing in Publication Data

Fenn, Richard
The dream of the perfect act: an enquiry
into the fate of religion in a secular
world.
1. Sociology, Christian
I. Title
261.1   BT738

ISBN 0–422–61300–2

Contents

Acknowledgments

This book makes it very clear how much I am indebted to the work of David Martin and Bryan Wilson. They also have provided collegial criticism and support, quite unfailingly, over many years; Graham Howes has been the source of extraordinarily helpful and careful comment on earlier portions of this book. I am very grateful to them, as I am to colleagues who have listened to parts of the argument developed here: Roland Robertson, Don Ploch, Ted Mills, Robert Friedrichs, James Beckford, Stephen Sykes, William Pickering, Eileen Barker, and Nikos Kokosalakis. For giving me an appreciation of the work of liturgical revision, I am particularly indebted to Leo Melenia and Dr George Cuming, who were especially generous in their assistance.

The work of putting together this manuscript over several years has required the incomparable secretarial and editorial help of Susan McLaughlin, whose patience survived several drafts without complaint until she saw the work done. Margaret and Mark Hodesh gave me a place in the Castine Inn from where I could prepare the final draft and survey the harbor, and always my wife Caroline accepted these distractions and encouraged the project. She joins me in thanking all those who have lent a hand.

Richard Fenn
Castine, Maine
September, 1986

The author and publishers would like to thank the following for their kind permission to quote copyright material: Aldine Publishing Company for an extract from *The Ritual Process: Structure and Anti-Structure* by Victor Turner; Anderson Publishing Company and Professor Richard Quinney for an extract from *Providence: The Reconstruction of Social and Moral Order* by Professor Quinney; Basil Blackwell Ltd for an extract from *Unholy Warfare: The Church and the Bomb* edited by D. Martin and P. Mullen; Collins Publishers for an extract from *Religion* by Leszek Kolakowski; The Free Press, a division of Macmillan, Inc., for extracts from *The Rules of Sociological Method* by Emile Durkheim, translated by Sarah A. Solovay and John H. Mueller and edited by George E.G. Catlin and from *Escape from Evil* by Ernest Becker; Harvard University Press for an extract from *Eleanor of Aquitaine and the Four Kings* by Amy Kelly; Johns Hopkins University Press for extracts from *Psychoanalytic Sociology: An Essay on the Interpretation of Historical Data and the Phenomena of Collective Behavior* by Fred Weinstein and Gerald Platt and from *Violence and the Sacred* by Rene Girard; A.R. Mowbray & Co. Ltd for an extract from *The Integrity of Anglicanism* by Stephen Sykes; W.W. Norton & Co., Inc. for an extract from *Adulthood*, ed. Eril Erikson. Oxford University Press for an extract from *Religion in Sociological Perspective* by Bryan Wilson; University of Chicago Press for an extract from *Talcott Parsons on Institutions and Social Evolution* by L. Mayhew; Van Gorcum for an extract from *A Language for Madness: The Abuse and Use of Christian Creeds* by H.F.G. Swanston.

Introduction

Religion carries many dreams: of glory and domination, of love and self-sacrifice, of surrender to mortality and victory over death. In this book I explore one such dream and its chances of fulfillment in large and complex societies. The dream, I argue, faces a most complex and intransigent world; its chances of fulfillment are scant; nonetheless, it will not easily die and may lead to profoundly disturbing social movements for national unity and glory before it perishes entirely.

The dream I will investigate involves action. Drawing on New Testament sources and the Christian tradition, I argue that Western religion carries the dream of the perfect act. What such perfection entails I will discuss in the first five chapters. There I speak of action as if it crosses various "thresholds" on the way toward perfection. The completed act combines will, meaning, and significance with consequences that are irreversible and extend to an entire social system.

I argue that the dream seems destined to be particularly frustrating and deceptive in modern societies. Their complexity makes it especially difficult for actions to be summarized in particular symbols that give them meaning or in signs that give them significance to a larger public. Problems of motivation are always difficult to resolve even with the best of intentions. These difficulties are compounded in modern societies, which offer multiple but limited contexts for action, distinguish private from public discourse, and lack a rhetoric for the most destructive or hateful impulses. Is there no vehicle for the religious dream even under these conditions?

To answer that question I turn to ritual. Surely, if there is any place where the religious dream either comes or at least rings true, it is in the performance of sacred rites. While I cannot begin to sample all modern liturgies, not to mention the secular rites of modern societies, I do focus on one set of rituals for the purpose of illustrating the barrier or impediments to acting out the religious dream. Even in such a favorable setting as contemporary churches, modern rites seem to replicate the very conditions which stand in the way of action in the larger society. My illustrations come largely from the rites of the Church of England as these have recently been revised. If a society as relatively homogeneous as the English nation finds it difficult to embody perfect action in its rites, how much more difficult it will be for the rites of smaller churches in larger, more complex societies to be vehicles for the religious dream on any but the most limited scale.

We need to appreciate the extraordinary achievements of highly ritualized societies if we are to know what, if anything, we may be missing now in the ways we have organized the process of growing up and growing old. The task of getting on with life in secular societies tends to spread out over many years rather than to culminate in crises at strategic moments in the person's lifetime. The energies and illusions of childhood are therefore carried forward, disguised, and allowed to be displaced on to a wide variety of activities where their effect may be relatively harmless, except where these energies and illusions strengthen myths of ethnic or national heroism and glory. Unless our collective life ends with a bang, therefore, we are more likely to end our individual lives with a whimper than with any ritualized transformation of the self. Those transformations are relatively few and idiosyncratic in secular societies; even modern rites of baptism, I will suggest in Chapter 4, leave many options open and questions therefore unanswered.

As Harrison (1962: xxx) observes, all rituals are rites of passage; only the particular transition varies from one rite to the next. Rituals have had the capacity to enable the individual to act out conflicting wishes and desires or to balance dread with hope as though the inherent conflict could be transcended in the end. The society's conflicts between paternal and maternal authority are experienced in ritual as individuals adopt costumes, follow leads, soar heavenward and ultimately sacrifice objects of their devotion. Ritual traces conflicting motives to a desire to retain old associations or recover lost attachments while moving ahead to new achievements or duties. By breaking those ties and providing lamentations suitable for the loss, ritual enables the individual to accept a new situation: a new birth, a new time of life, a new status in the community. By surrounding this passage with certain requirements and protections the community also safeguards its own institutions for another generation.

Rituals enable the self to undergo a passage from the old self to the new; that requires self-sacrifice, and yet such sacrifice enables the self to become a more effective and significant actor in the larger society. Mixed with earth and dust, the self must be transformed if it is to fly, light as air, to inhabit the world of the "deathless ones." Only those who dance with powerful figures, with figures of power, can take such a flight (*Parabola* VI, 3, 1981: 3). According to the Daedalus myth, Icarus, who does not properly join with his father in a ritual dance, loses his power of flight, dies submerged in the element of water, and is buried in the earth once and for all. In a highly ritualized society the self is made real through successive transformations: from an earthly to a spiritual substance; from child to adult; from being ordinary to being possessed; from being one possessed to one made new; from being made new to being at one with the very old and the ancestors. The self proceeds, not through a gradual process that has no beginning, no sharp stages, and no end, but through ritualized transformations.

The succession through stages in life is quite different in a modern society as compared with a simpler, more traditional one. In the modern a person's development from birth through death to beyond is little more than a series of "developmental" periods in the individual's life (see Erikson 1977, Loevinger 1976, Levinson 1978). The old is no longer brought forward into the new by a change in the essence of the self. The child may therefore not wholly surrender magical, egocentric, or grandiose ideas about the self in exchange for more limited self-conceptions. Magical thinking may therefore appear in the modern adult as an exaggerated sense of one's own impact on others; egocentricity simply becomes an absorption in one's own growth and potential; a sense of being unbounded be- · comes a feeling that one has limitless possibilities or responsibilities (Lifton 1967). Moods may therefore swing with the stock-market or with the fate of celebrities, with the unemployment rate or the rate of inflation. In a modern society there are few rites that require of us the radical transformation of the old self. What the child once wore only as a mask of adulthood later becomes an illusion about the self. Only an undue seriousness remains to warn others, if not oneself, that the old is present within and under the form of the new. But in the more ritualized societies, as with the sacramental notion of the transubstantiation of bread and wine into Christ's "Body and Blood," the new appears within and under the form of the old as the latter's new essence.

To enter the future without abandoning or being held back by the past requires that cherished associations be brought forward into a time and place where parents and ancestors have never been. Rituals in traditional societies could enable a community to carry the past in to the future while opening the gates to new life. In rites of initiation, for instance, the young not only entered into the life of the tribe but through symbolic death achieved a lasting closeness with the tribe's ancestors; no wonder that metaphors of death and gestures of sacrifice accompanied such initiation.

We now know from many sources that, for those who take part in a rite of initiation, "death" is powerfully metaphoric. The old self "dies" that a new one can be born. The new self takes on the life of those who have gone before, wears their clothes, grasps their relics and their faith. Jane Harrison gives us a succinct but stunning reminder of the metaphoric "life and death" character of rites of transition in tribal societies: "a man dies socially when he ceases to be able to dance his tribal dances" (Harrison 1962: xxxii). That statement may fit the reality of tribal societies; the question is whether it can be restated in a form that will lead us to the truth of modern societies.

When the life of the community is essential to the life of the individual, to live outside the community is to risk not merely ostracism and "social death" but one's very life. The point comes home if we look at a particular word for the mature, "grown up," fully initiated individual: it is *teleios*, (Harrison 1962: xxxii). To take on the garments, the life and work of one's ancestors means to become complete. The same sense of the word *teleios*, according to one authority on biblical literature, applies to Jesus in the Gospels, where the term means to be completely and perfectly human (see Robinson 1950, 1957). We can now understand why the Jews of the time thought it scandalous that a man could be whole, perfected, and complete who was denied the rites of his people in death and who, in life, chose a maverick rite of baptism in the desert rather than the perfection offered by the temple. To live and die outside the camp and yet to be perfect, complete, and whole was thus a contradiction in terms. Outside the community, so to speak, there can be no such transformation. That is one truth, theologically speaking, to which I adhere. As a sociologist, however, I am aware that various social realities will make it virtually impossible for individuals to become authentic actors whose deeds have clear and enduring meaning for themselves and for others. This book is one attempt to clarify the social realities that impede our realization of what I take to be religious truth.

When one generation succeeds to the position and authority of another in a traditional and relatively simple society, the difference between two generations disappears. The young wear the garments and insignia of their elders while the older generation passes on its gifts of knowledge and power. The younger generation abandons, sacrifices, and offers its own distinctions, while the older generation prepares to move aside or yield its positions and authority. Nonetheless, the older generation claims the right to demand loyalty to its values and symbols, and the price of receiving the inheritance is a continued obedience to traditional authority. Conversely, to acquire the authority of the elders the younger generation agrees to a certain loss of identity within the community – a willingness, for instance, to work within a framework that defines what is worth discovering and dying for. Even in a modern society, rites of graduation ensure that the violence done to the younger generation's identity will be more symbolic than real and that the authority of the elders will be passed on without violence. But the solemnity and elaborate justifications even for academic ritual indicate that there may well be unconscious murder afoot. I will take up the question of unconscious motives and conscious intentions in Chapter 3.

Even in a complex society there are very real costs in leaving behind certain attachments and pursuing more distant or symbolic goals. It is costly for parents to train their children to lead lives in which the parents cannot directly share. It is costly to accept chronic disenchantment, however mild, with the appearances and rewards of social life. It is costly to go through motions that no longer express genuine feelings and call for commitment. It is costly to live without common goals and aspirations. In a social crisis, as it is with individuals undergoing crises in identity, a larger proportion of individuals may become unwilling to go through certain motions and to speak in prescribed ways without "meaning it" (Erikson 1958: 70 ff.).

Unresolved ties to people or places or to a way of life can prevent individuals from "getting on with it" and from acquiring new skills or satisfactions in life. In their study of working-class men from the Boston area Sennett and Cobb (1966) repeatedly found individuals who despised their current work and surroundings despite the fact that these individuals had made very real progress in the form of additional education, of income, or of attainments in their jobs. Their lack of satisfaction became apparent as they reminisced about their parents' work. By comparison with their parents' labors, what they were now doing did not seem to be "real" work. Sometimes they looked on themselves as a sham or as not "having what it takes"; their origins, a family or community that they still held dear, were more real to them than their present social life in a college or middle-class suburb.

Finally, then, the small ceremonies that bind individuals together into a moral community of mutual respect, if not affection, may become so formal or fragile that they appear to be a sham or an imposition; they are thus easily ignored or broken. Individuals are thus left to their own devices to make up for their lost but still precious associations. Some yearning may take on the form of romantic seeking for lost loves. Some will turn to activities that promise a more concrete and direct connection with an object of desire: witness many a commercial that promises real connection and final release from the burdens of separate existence in an orgy of fun and convivial drinking. Under these conditions it is difficult to see how a secularized society can bind people together into valued associations whose memories and hopes for progress transcend death.

While primitive societies enjoy rituals that can transform decline, loss and even death into sources of renewal and life, "modern" societies have less obvious need for such rituals of recovery and transformation. In a society without enduring and intense ties between individuals, a rite will simply reflect the transient and distant relationships among the urbane. A confession of sin will be economical in its expression of penitence, since little in the way of grief or grievance may have occurred among those who still gather at the major liturgical service of the week. Affection and loyalty to the larger society will find little expression in the prayers of thanksgiving or the prayers of the faithful. Rather, prayers for *categories* of citizens ("laborers, those in authority," etc.) replace the naming of the Queen or President, and hopes will be expressed for generalized harmony rather than for the redress of specific grievances or for the growth of specifically Christian virtues in the body politic. Cool, concise, and abstract relationships find expression in appropriate liturgies.

When prayers take on an abstract quality, as the faithful pray for categories of citizens and workers, the actual persons being prayed for or remembered become lost. Although some modern rites provide blanks where specific names can be mentioned, the format of the text suggests that the names are interchangeable and their choice optional or even arbitrary. When those who have died in the service of a nation or community cannot be recovered in vital ritual or rejoined on a last great day, something has indeed been lost.

This book continues the on-going sociological concern with the secularization of the modern world. To give an account of the process by which the sacred becomes more malleable and less immune to criticism and change has been the task of sociology from the outset; I am simply writing in that tradition. To modify the rites by which literally millions of people worship is perhaps the most radical of efforts to defend the sacred against the competition of the modern world; it is therefore paradoxical that it should also represent a profoundly radical step toward further secularization. What is lost in that process is the sense that reality, however much it unfolds over time and however much humans cooperate in making that reality, somehow transcends both history and the individual. The secular world, as West (1978) reminds us, pays a price for making humans the measure of all things; that price is to lose contact with Being itself.

The realist tradition in sociology defends the truth question against mere considerations of "alternative realities." In these pages I have a strong but implicit debt to the work not only of the sociological realists but to social critics who believe that there *are* universal laws at work in social life. I am particularly in debt to the work of Herbert Read, who was profoundly sociological in assessing the social conditions under which individuals in general, and artists in particular, shape reality, and who insisted that the truth question goes well beyond the question of how reality is shaped and made. If reality is to be manufactured without distorting the truth, he argued, it will be made only under conditions in which individuals are wholly free and yet wholly members of autonomous and closely-knit groups – hardly a description of the clients of church bureaucracies or the denizens of new estates. Herbert Read was a critic who drew not only on the anarchist tradition but on psychoanalysis, in describing and criticizing the repressive aspects of normal, everyday social life. (His remarks on the pathological aspects of normalcy were directed primarily at British society, but they can be translated with no loss of meaning to the American context.) If experience is the basis on which individuals and groups measure their satisfaction with certain social innovations, that experience itself is useful only to the extent that it is free, self-determining, open to suggestion from the unconscious, and based on social relationships that embody the values used for assessing and measuring what is fitting and useful. Otherwise the shape and content of social rituals will become as artificial, obsolescent, and deceptively attractive as the products Herbert Read once found characteristic of a capitalist economy.

The sociological attack on pragmatism as a secularizing distortion of social reality continued on this side of the Atlantic in the work of Parsons and, perhaps more accessibly, in the critique of pragmatism by Mills (1966). From time to time in this work I draw heavily on Mills's criticism of pragmatism, but I would like to note here its immediate relevance to the task in hand; that is, of giving a sociological account of a major change in the rites by which a national church expresses itself in common worship. One key to the criticism is Mills's discussion of the pragmatists' notion of action, and I will introduce that discussion here in some detail.

To put it simply, Mills finds fault with Dewey for drastically oversimplifying the highly political or bureaucratic context in which modern individuals primarily live and work. Mills notes that, "To realize pragmatism's model of action, a segment of behavior has to unfold slowly, take up one thing at a time, be in continuity with the past" (Mills 1966: 393). It would be hard to find a better description of the work of the Liturgical Commission in England. That group *did* take up one thing at a time: one change in wording in one prayer at a time, and eventually one aspect of a proposed revision at a time: for example, a creed or the collects. That action was "in continuity with the past," since the Commission spent considerable effort to find historical precedent for its suggested revisions, and its work indeed unfolded slowly over the better part of two decades; even that work, moreover, was simply the final stage in the work of revision that had begun in the liturgical movement late in the nineteenth century. Contrast this disciplined inquiry, which like the work of a scientist in a laboratory proceeds with caution while accumulating results slowly in piecemeal fashion over time, with the discordant facts of modern social life: violence, disaster, the mobilization of political groups around specific party lines, the imposition of political creeds, and the rigid administrative implementation of executive orders or of statutes in tightly coordinated organizations. As Mills notes of Dewey's view of action, it is not political and fits "conduct that makes decisions about situations that have not been regulated" (pp. 392–93). Certainly force and regulation were in the background of the Liturgical Commission; the liturgy was legally imposed and the Church's bureaucracy heavily involved in its development. In foreground, however, were simply scholars and church leaders discussing one alternative at a time in the light of historical precedent and current options. Those proceedings exemplify what Dewey had in mind when speaking of "action"; as Mills put it, such action is "the conduct of an individual in non-rationalized spheres or types of society" (pp. 392–93).

Under these conditions, it is not surprising that the Liturgical Commission proceeded with a pragmatist's notion of what action entails, but from Mills's sociological viewpoint such pragmatism provides only a very falsified consciousness of the larger social context in which the Church as a whole, and its Commissioners in particular, were in fact situated. In the Church of England, for instance, the litany offers prayers for many things, and one of them is for divine protection from famine. In the prayers for the ordination of a bishop, many of those prayers from the litany are used, but a few are omitted; among those omitted is the prayer for protection from famine. Famine is not likely, perhaps, to come to a bishop's attention, whose job is to teach or administer – actions in which pragmatism may be more useful than heroic or drastic action.

In the American Episcopal Church there was a similar feeling that prayers for divine protection "against the dangers of this night" were out of place in a world made safe for pedestrians by electricity. Indeed, the Standing Liturgical Commission decided that the American Episcopal Church is now living in a different "culture" than the one in which the *Book of Common Prayer* was first written (1662) and cited a number of sociological factors to make their point. For instance, the Commission thought liturgical references to "foe" or "peril" were out of place in a world where dangers are more general or abstract and city streets are lighted at night by electricity (Liturgical Commission, Memo 9, June 1970: 3, 35–36). This reflects a consciousness, clearly false, of the larger social context of the Church, but it makes sense when one thinks of Liturgical Commissions carefully going about their work in a spirit of inquiry and judicious experimentation. The point is that pragmatism describes the way the Church, in its liturgical experimentation, both thought and worked; it would not be surprising, therefore, for the new rites themselves to exhibit the pragmatist's notion of action.

Although it would not be surprising for the form and content of the new rites to exhibit pragmatism's assumptions, it would be unfortunate, since the world as a whole is not composed "of liberal individuals heavily endowed with substantive rationality" (Mills 1966: 393). For such "liberal individuals" it makes sense to introduce "trial" liturgies. That pragmatist orientation, I will later argue, subverts the nature of the liturgy, which is itself a mock trial and puts on trial the authorities of the Church and of the world. There the world comes to judgment; hardly possible when it is the liturgy itself which is "on trial." It makes sense for liberal individuals to consider a variety of options, and it follows that they would embody these options in the final form of the new rites. However, it subverts the external, imposing, obligatory, and constraining nature of the truth for its statements to be reduced to a series of options that depend on convenience. To apply Durkheim's (1982) judgment on pragmatism to this result of liturgical revision, one might say that the effort to give liturgical shape to reality undermined the liturgy's ability to give truth its shape. The "shape of the liturgy" therefore conforms more largely to the social context of the Church's Commissions than it does to the truth which transcends both history and the individual. In Durkheimian terms, then, the new rites give the most secular shape to the most sacred of institutions.

Perhaps the most sympathetic of Mills's perceptions of pragmatism is found in this description; speaking of the pragmatist's view of action, he writes: "It can be experimental ... because it trusts the grand direction of the underlying patterns of change" (Mills 1966: 393).

In this work I am investigating acts. They are a species of what Durkheim used to call "social facts." They are facts, and therefore they have a certain reality that is not to be minimized by calling it "merely social." On the contrary, because the facts are social, they are anchored in an order that is not simply artificial and arbitrary but natural, according to Durkheim. On the other hand, as a social fact, an act is manufactured out of the material of social interaction. Like history, acts unfold and take shape in more or less continuity with the past – sometimes more but sometimes less continuity, according to the kind of interaction in which acts are manufactured. Acts may incorporate precisely what, as Mills points out, the pragmatists tend to obscure: the role of brute force or of violence and of sudden, decisive moves that interrupt the careful. The idea of an act, I will argue, moves beyond the arguments between sociology and pragmatism to a point at which certain critical questions, crucial to an understanding of the process of secularization, will easily be posed. At the very least, the notion of an act transcends the dichotomies that characterize the thought of sociological realism and pragmatism alike: thought versus action, individual versus society, means versus ends, goals versus values, behavior versus environment.

Take, for example, the notion of the "act of hunting" as compared simply with hunting as a kind of action. Left in the hands of pragmatist thought, hunting is a prototypical form of inquiry: behavior leading to the satisfaction of hunger, to survival, to adaptation to the environment and perhaps greater control over the environment (Mills 1966: 378–80). From the viewpoint of pragmatism, hunting as a set of actions may lead to thoughtful reflection on how to improve one's weapons, perhaps, or one's ability to track animals, or even to improve the supply of animals through careful culling of the herd. Pragmatism might be equally disposed, however, to think of hunting as the empirical test or verification of certain ideas; certainly Durkheim ([1955], 1982: 5) faults Peirce for such a utilitarian notion of belief as having meaning only in terms of its consequences and the actions to which it gives rise. As an "act" rather than as action, however, hunting is a form of behavior in which thought is embedded quite literally at every step; it is clearly an intellectual activity which symbolically acts out (and not merely models or represents) a series of actions and social interactions. This is not to say that one cannot isolate for analytical purposes certain ideas and actions or investigate the time and place or the order and sequence in which they appear. It is to say, however, that one can fully give a sociological account of hunting only as an act in which the dichotomy between thought and action disappears.

Hunting is a particularly useful example of a prototypical social act because it was perhaps the first human action to be embodied in a ritual; certainly it has been argued that the first ritual enacted hunting (Burkert 1979). In the form of a rite, hunting unites what is individual in the process of hunting with what is undeniably social; how, indeed, could one separate the two in the course of the rite itself? The rite makes hunting an act in which the means coincide with the end: the taking of animal life. The end, furthermore, is not merely a "goal" which can be reached according to means that are more or less rational; it is a goal that is simultaneously a value – perhaps the supreme value in the life of the community; for example, control over life and death. No wonder that Mills was so critical of Dewey for reducing hunting to a form of behavior and for seeing action as a practical activity oriented toward survival; action is always and everywhere more or less oriented toward values and not only toward certain objectifiable goals; indeed, it is this "more or less" that makes a comparative and historical approach to social institutions both possible and necessary (as compared with Dewey's abstract, formal, and evolutionary perspective; see Mills, 1966: 379–80). Where thought and action are so intertwined, furthermore, the right way to think is acted out and the right kind of action is expressed in gesture, word, and symbol: an order that is both social and so inevitable and right as to be "natural." The truth question is answered even as it is asked in a rite that manufactures the social act, say, of hunting.

It is important that Durkheim had to criticize the pragmatists for failing to separate the question of truth from the question of reality. From an evolutionary perspective that focuses on the continuity of action with inquiry, it may be easy to ignore the discontinuity between society and nature. As Mills (1966: 381) points out, Dewey in fact considered both nature and society to be the "environment" to action – hardly a term that leads one to notice any discontinuity between the two. It was that discontinuity, however, which precisely concerned Durkheim, who found that such a separation in thought led Nietzsche to see notions of cause and effect and ideas about social categories as mere fictions; that is why Nietzsche affirmed action over thought and decision over the suspension of judgment in various analyses (see Durkheim [1955], 1982: 3). Here, then, is the paradox which sociology consistently addresses. On the one hand, to confuse society with nature makes it possible to elide the question of truth into the question of reality. They are not the same, as Durkheim found it necessary to remind the pragmatists; and Mills made essentially the same criticism of Dewey. On the other hand, if one does distinguish society adequately from nature, it is possible to reduce society and its notions to mere fiction while affirming only brute drive and will; a fault that Durkheim quickly found in Nietzsche. Durkheim wanted to make the truth social (and not metaphysical), but he wanted to make the social true (not merely artificial but rational and natural). As Allcock puts it in his introduction to Durkheim's lectures on pragmatism: "In Durkheim's view, only a sociological theory of truth can explain this double nature" (in Durkheim [1955], 1982: xiv).

If sociology were theology, I would have no difficulty in agreeing with Durkheim. No act, however, has ever fully elided the distinction between society and nature; the truth question will always arise, even in a rite that fulfills all the conditions necessary for a social act. The act of hunting, even though it was ritualized, did not lay to rest the question of truth; otherwise there would have been no need for further accounts to arise in the form of myth. Myth, and later, religion, is the institution which marks the separation of reality from truth and of society from nature. That is why, I would argue, the myth of the Garden of Eden notes the existence of two trees: one of the knowledge of good and evil and the other of life itself. The existence of these two trees allows the truth question to be asked, but it is the serpent, of course, who asks it.

1
The Perfect Act: A Brief Introduction to Religious Hope in a Modern World

The "act" is what Durkheim would call a "social fact": an aspect of reality that is not reducible or even easily comparable to anything else. Indeed, I am arguing that the "act" is a primary fact of social life; it is necessary, although hardly sufficient, if social life is ever to move beyond what is immediate and temporary to something that has at least a little continuity. Without the "act", *per se*, all that is left for social life to ponder is a series of actions in which one leads to another without continuity and without any real distinction. In the absence of the act, one might go through the motion of giving or receiving a name, of being pronounced dead or installed as a leader; no one would know when, however, the deed was done, the name given, or the leader finally installed. The "act" gives definition to social life that no number of actions can accomplish. That is why I consider it the prototypical social fact.

In a modern society it is difficult to find a complete act. In a somewhat more limited sense, of course, we are familiar with legislative or judicial acts. In this chapter I will suggest why even these enactments are not in themselves complete acts, as I will define the term. They are actions completed into acts as far as the institutional context of the court or legislature permits; the full range of the act, as I will define it, remains to be seen. I will point to the will behind the act as well as its meaning, its interpretations and reception by others, and its societal consequences as essential aspects of the "act" taken as a whole. If an act is difficult to find or to recognize in all its aspects in modern societies, that difficulty is an important indicator of what makes these societies particularly "modern." Indeed, I am taking the incompleteness of acts as a crucially important characteristic of modern societies. As with many sociological concepts, there is the germ of a theory planted in the concept of the act. By saying that the act is a prototypical social fact or essential aspect of social life, I am suggesting that without the act a social system, of whatever size or complexity, could not develop (although it might continue on some other basis, e.g. force alone). That is a rudimentary theory, but there it is. When Durkheim wrote about the act of signing a contract, for instance, he was suggesting that this act is so important that without some equivalent ability of making a promise and of making such a promise stick, society – as compared with some transient or chaotic social life – would have been virtually impossible. I agree.

The notion of an act that I wish to develop here is not only an embryonic theory but very hypothetical. The "act" is not to be confused, as I have suggested, with an Act of some legislative body; certainly it is far more than is suggested in phrases relating to the theater (a fine act; Act 1) or to the dramas of everyday life (what an act!). My sociological notion of an act also goes well beyond the level of opinion that a particular action is, for instance, an act of kindness or courage. Let us go back, for a moment, to the example just given in the preceding paragraph: the act of signing a contract. To the commonsense eye, that is all there is to it; one makes a promise, signs a document, and perhaps puts up collateral or provides at least a witness to the deed. To the sociological eye, however, there are aspects of this act that are no less important for being invisible. As Durkheim noted, without a wide range of shared values – for example, the value placed on rationality or truth-telling – the contract as such would be impossible. What makes the action of signing a contract an *act* is not usually stated even in the fine print. Without certain shared values the act would have no meaning, and to break the promise would have few consequences. Even without the consequences, some of them stated in the contract, others stated in the law, and still other consequences left unstated but widely assumed on the basis of these shared values, the contractual act would not be complete. A full account of the action of signing a contract therefore requires a far more expanded and hypothetical notion of the contract as an act, a social fact with many parts, of which only a few are visible or immediately knowable. It therefore will be difficult to verify the statements that I am about to make about the nature of an act. In focusing on religious ritual, however, I have chosen an area where most, if not all, the aspects of an act can usually be found intact and together. If some aspects of the concept of the act cannot be located even there, the problem may lie with the concept itself; on the other hand, the rite in question may be faulty. Only a theory can help to tell whether it is the concept or the ritual that is lacking.

Some of these introductory points that I am making may seem like unnecessary intellectual flourishes, but take something like an ordinary, everyday act: an act of self-sacrifice. For the philosopher such an act may or may not pose a problem of recognition. The pragmatist Peirce, for instance, argued that one could not recognize an act of self-sacrifice "if no such thing as self-sacrifice exists" (in Mills 1966: 202). For Mills, however, a simple philosophic realism was not sufficient; the social fact cannot be defined as such in terms of some putative abstract or eternal idea. Not dwelling in the realm of Platonic absolutes, the sociologist casts around for a social context which gives rise to the act of self-sacrifice and to which the act of self-sacrifice also gives rise. As Mills noted of Peirce, his notion of a society was so abstract, indefinite, and hypothetical as to require faith alone rather than sight; the more concrete or limited a social context, the more Peirce thought it distorted the truth with strategic or competitive interests and opened the door to the merely practical or even the greedy consideration (Mills 1966: 203ff.). For the sociologist the answer to the question of what constitutes an act of self-sacrifice can only be found in delimited social contexts, precisely where different and even opposing acts are likely to occur. There is a strong but secularized version of the Christian faith here in Mills's preference for the real to be found in the midst of whatever is concrete, social, and therefore flawed; it is worth taking a moment to make that faith more explicit.

In Durkheim's lectures on pragmatism we can find what I would call a sociologist's version of the Incarnation. For Durkheim any act, including an act of self-sacrifice, is an essential social fact; it is social fact, moreover, that "makes societies, although it could equally well be said that it also derives from them" (Durkheim [1955], 1982: 97). Durkheim speaks of the truth as social; it is therefore often complex, abstract, beyond our immediate experience. On the other hand, the truth, according to Durkheim, is also so human that it "thus comes closer to us, rather than moves away and disappears in the distant realms of an intelligible world or divine understanding" (p. 97). No sanctified reason approachable only by the most context-free or alienated of intellectuals provides the embodiment of truth for the sociologists: "It [the truth] is no doubt superior to individual consciousness; but even the collective element in it exists only through the consciousness of individuals, and truth is only achieved by individuals" (p. 97).

Of course, for Durkheim no society is perfect, and individual consciousness is always distorted both by its context and by the individual's own desires, which are too often infinite or, conversely, too often crushed by social burdens. Even when the weight of a society is moderate, its demands may be confusing, inconsistent, and incomplete. No doubt, then, that for the truth to be social, to be human and apparent to the individual, is to involve both the society and the individual in a fallen world. The truth has been made flesh and dwelt among us, and we have seen the truth – so goes the Durkheimian creed. That truth, however, is badly scarred, and we can know it only partially by sight – so goes the confession. If we know an act of self-sacrifice when we see one, then it is not because we are party to some abstract idea. We can know an act of self-sacrifice when we see one because we know that individuals can embody – and also give themselves to – societies: that the values they hold dear come from beyond them, in the larger society, and yet come alive only through their personal commitment and conduct. In this incarnation of the truly social and the truly personal, society itself becomes human and draws close to us as does no other reality. The overtones of Christian doctrine in this secular, sociological affirmation are unmistakable.

Like the Incarnation, the act itself is complete but can only be known in the light of further interpretations, understandings, and consequences. Whether or not an act is one of self-sacrifice depends on many factors that are only anticipated at the time of the deed itself. The meaning of the deed and its later interpretation and consequences are what a theologian might call proleptically present in self-sacrifice. The gratitude and enrichment or renewal of the larger society come later, however much they were anticipated or even intended in the original action. That is why, as a sociologist, I defined the act as including the acquisition of meaning, eventual public reception, and final societal consequences. From the theological point of view, the Incarnation is an act that is still continuing in the life of those who understand, receive, and act out the significance of the actions coded in the New Testament; indeed, some of the consequences of the actions of Jesus (e.g. the coming together of a witnessing community) are considered theologically to be part of the act of the Incarnation itself. It is in that sense that I consider what seems empirically separable (e.g. initial deed and later interpretation or consequence) as part of the notion of the act. Of course, an action may be self-sacrificing without being an act of self-sacrifice. To become the latter the society in which the action takes place must understand its meaning, and those who are more distant beneficiaries must respond in ways that are signaled by the initial action. In the absence of such later response and affirmation, the initial action may not be noticed, or even seen as self-sacrificing; it might escape notice entirely or be misunderstood. So it was with what theologians call the Incarnation.

The search for the perfect act is no doubt religious; it is also the holy grail of a Durkheimian sociology. Marx, on the other hand, understood that no matter how many people participate, for instance, in the building of a society, the end result has not been what anyone fully intended, and Weber developed the doctrine of "unintended consequences" into a tragic principle inherent in history itself (see Genth and Mills, 1958: 45-50). Whereas both Marx and Weber might agree that thought *per se* is neither intelligible nor complete until it issues in action, neither would place pragmatic criteria (e.g. of utility, convenience, or satisfaction) in the place of sociological criteria for analyzing the truth of an idea. On the contrary, Marx understood that false consciousness would make it virtually inevitable for notions of utility and satisfaction to be distorted; no act could therefore be an expression of the truth in a world in which class conflict distorts interpretations, disguises interests, and diverts action toward consequences that make even revolutionary actions difficult, if not impossible, to consummate. There is an eschatology in both Marxist and Christian thought that is notably missing in Durkheim. Weber also lacks an eschatology, although he does employ a tragic notion of irreversible and unintended consequences. In the notion of the act that I am proposing, therefore, I intend to provide as full a definition as possible without making the assumption that all defining elements can be found in any particular social context; if they are missing, and some elements always are lacking, their absence will call for an explanation. To provide one is the purpose of the later accounts that I shall offer of why even acts intended to be complete (e.g. the most formal of religious rites) are flawed.

The similarities between the religious and sociological notions of the perfect act may be quite apparent, especially when we consider the ideal-typical act and the notion of the Incarnation. What are we to make, however, of the disparities and the contradictions that inevitably enter into the unfolding of an act's meaning and consequences within the context of history, where perfection may be hidden for the time being and unfold only slowly in the light of interpretations and consequences that could only be prefigured at a particular moment? A Durkheimian sociology and the Christian notion of the Incarnation therefore agree to this extent: that motive, intention, purpose, meaning, public significance, and societal consequence cohere in the nature of the whole and completed act. What, then, do the two make of the course of history in which these elements become separated? Is that course a progressive fall from a state of grace or, on the contrary, is it a fulfillment of what was latent in the act itself?

Durkheim is clear that there is something providential about the course of history; we are therefore not to despise these later elements of contradiction or inconsistency that emerge as what was once interrelated becomes parceled out into separate corners of society. He uses the example of the family, which once was a unit that had legal, political, and economic aspects as well as communal or familial functions to perform; it is no decline from a state of initial grace to find that the law, the state, and the economy now perform these duties for society, duties once housed under the roof, so to speak, of a family unit. On the contrary, the earlier social state was one of confusion rather than homogeneity; confusion of elements that can and eventually should be distinguished.

Furthermore, as distinctions become visible between, say, the law and the family, each aspect becomes better able to perform its function. The law is better able to be the law when separated from the family, and so is the economy. The emergence of distinctions between what was initially confused therefore enables the sociologist to "follow the natural articulations of each thing" (Durkheim [1955], 1982: 96). In answer to the possible criticism of these later forms as fixed and therefore as static and resistant to further progress,

Durkheim argues that such fixity can represent an achievement that should be historically fixed and solid. History can occasionally "rest on its laurels," he argues, since the products of change may indeed be a fulfillment of what was present at earlier stages of history ([1915], 1965: 96). This is a familiar argument, in which change becomes progress, and progress becomes development or fulfillment according to whether or not the end-state is latent as a potentiality or intention at the outset, and other sociologists have rightly been critical of its religious and secular assumptions (see Nisbet 1969). No doubt it represents a sociological view of history as providentially guided or disposed if not wholly sacred in itself. Here, however, I am concerned not with debunking the pretensions of this sociological view but with exposing the logic of its understanding of the act. How does such a view of history elaborate what is involved in the notion of the act itself?

Consider, as the first step toward understanding the notion of the act under the auspices of a divine or secular providence, the first threshold that action must cross: the threshold of the will. In the beginning, as it were, is both motive and intention. The motive is precisely what moves the individual to any action. It may be any one of the wide range of motives with which we are familiar from psychoanalytic thought; take, for example, a desire for fusion between the self and another (see Silverman, Lachmann, and Milich 1982). That motive may initiate an action, such as a gesture of greeting, or the bobbing in rhythm to a common beat, or even a detailed letter expressing affection or some grievance. The intention might be to communicate, whether about mutual differences or about what one has in common; the motive, as I have mentioned, may be to reinforce the illusion that one is literally "at one" with another person. Psychoanalytic understanding and method may help in diagnosing the relation between motive and intention; it certainly is the purpose of any phenomenological approach to grasp the relation between the two from the standpoint of what is experienced by the individual engaging in the action. The fact that Western culture has developed intellectual and therapeutic disciplines that specialize in an understanding of the first threshold which action must cross, indicates the extent to which modern societies have "developed." This progress, however, opens up wide areas of disagreement; for instance, on whether an action is self-sacrificing and even on whether such self-sacrifice is rational, voluntary, and conscious rather than driven by a latent will to obliterate the self in union, say, with the mother. Although the perfect act leaves no room for doubt on the relation of motive to intention, most actors are only partly acquainted with the springs of their action and find themselves inconsistent or vague in articulating their intentions. A sociology that attempts to give a full account of the individual's will therefore requires the services of a psychoanalytic or phenomenological viewpoint.

Religion may provide its own myth to account for disparities or gaps in the relation of motive to intention. Popular religion notes that hell is paved with good intentions – pavement that covers the not-so-good motive that underlies the best of intentions. Until recently, the Anglican communion found it necessary to state, in a general confession of sin, that individuals had transgressed in "the devices and desires of our own hearts," an inward sinfulness far below the level of intention and beneath the reach of ordinary consciousness. Recent revision of this confession emphasizes sin at the level of consciousness, a failure in "thought, word, and deed" to love God and neighbor, but it acknowledges that sin may be "unknown" as well as known. Of course, sin may be unknown because it operates at the level of one's deepest motivation; that is why the older version argued that "there is no health in us"; the recent version accounts for that possibility as a simple failure of the individual to be aware of his or her sin. The ability of any religion to give a full account of what is lacking or discordant in an act does depend on the extent to which its rites can embody the complete dimensions of a perfect act; on that point, of course, I will have more to say throughout this book.

Here it is enough to note that religion may – or may not – stress the heart, the "*nous*," the inward motive that, unknown to the individual, may define the nature of an act in the eyes of God. That divine judgment, of course, takes everything into account, even if it must wait until the last day to do so. In the meantime, a ritual, in setting forth dimensions of a complete act, may be able to anticipate that final judgment in ways that will drive the individual or group to get their act together. What appeared to an individual to be an act of self-sacrifice may, as a result of participation in a rite, seem to have been less sacrificial than self-serving or self-destructive. A rite may intensify an individual's awareness of the relation between motive and intention that must be completed if "will" is to emerge in action.

I will argue that secularization has thus reduced religion's authority to define the expression of human motives in specific actions. Certainly individuals can find outside the churches ample roles and identities for their own use and consumption. The public sphere has enlarged to make room for expressive activities from football to modern dance, from street demonstrations to political campaigns. The decline of sacred authority, with the resulting variety of public masks and identities, makes possible an unprecedented freedom, even a degree of license, in the publication of human motives and intentions. The controlled performance of the sacrament that both expresses and disguises powerful motives of love and hatred has yielded to a carnival atmosphere in the public sphere. That the public expression of motives has discarded the mask of religion is no secret; what this development means for the individual's ability to complete and perfect action is one focus of this inquiry.

As the boundaries set by the Church on the recognition or acting out of human impulses begin to erode, what once was regarded as demonic finds esthetic expression. Individuals experiment with prohibited feelings and find satisfaction in what once was illicit or simply in poor taste. As Bell points out, liberation from the Church's restraints and the discovery of esthetic freedoms follow a loss of fear of eternal damnation (see Dobbelaere 1981: 88). But Bell's picture of the resurgence of the sacred, in the form of hitherto disguised motives and impulses, may well exaggerate the degrees of freedom open to the ordinary person in modern societies. Wilson argues very forcefully that daily life in the modern world is impoverished and self-defeating because it lacks what I would call a rhetoric of acts; at least:

"Religious perceptions and goals, religiously induced sensitivities, religiously inspired morality, and religious socialization appear to be of no immediate relevance to the operation of the modern social system ... Planning, not revelation; rational order, not inspiration; systematic routine, not charismatic or traditional action, are the imperatives in ever widening arenas of public life."
(Wilson 1982: 176–77)

Wilson also reminds us that the achieving of spiritual heights by a religious élite always has the effect of secularizing daily life for ordinary individuals who cannot find in such rarefied religious teaching a rhetoric for the expression of their deepest motives and most fearful impulses (p. 173). To make spiritual achievements the privilege of an esthetic élite would not enlighten the individual cursed with bureaucratic routines and highly limited responsibilities. That life, governed by the requirements of a specialized ordering of work and even of less formal activities, hardly sanctifies the full range of human motives. Nothing less than a total scope for the play and redemption of human motive, however, can constitute salvation; on that point Wilson is very clear indeed (p. 175). *For three reasons, then, religion may no longer provide a rhetoric for translating personal motives and intentions into acts: (1) other cultural sources provide such publicity; (2) religion is too élite an exercise to be expressive for the ordinary individual; (3) religion per se has no bearing on everyday life.*

2

The second threshold which action must cross on the way toward becoming a completed act is that of others' perception. In crossing the first threshold, others' perceptions do matter and come significantly into play, if only in anticipation; but in crossing the second threshold, however, others' perceptions are decisive. They determine how the purpose of an action will be related to others' purposes; that relation will constitute its meaning. By purpose, I refer to an actor's motives and intentions as these are combined in a will for those toward whom the action is directed. The will of an individual now becomes the purpose as it is communicated to others who are the intended recipients of the action. Take again the example of self-sacrifice. "Sacrifice sales" advertise sacrificial purposes in such a way as to remind customers of the benefits they are about to receive. That audience, however, may hear a "sacrificial" sale and think instead of the warning, *caveat emptor*, according to their own self-regarding purposes. Purpose only coheres entirely when an act is complete at the second threshold; then its meaning becomes clear.

Religious ritual has crucial functions to play precisely at this threshold; that is, in ensuring that the purpose of an action will become meaningful to all who are involved as actors, beneficiaries, and witnesses. Take, for example, an account from the New Testament. In the account of the meeting between disciples and a stranger on the road to Emmaus, it is clear that a radical doubt has emerged among the disciples over the meaning of the crucifixion. The stranger describes the purpose of the action in terms of prophecies that could supply its meaning; the purpose of the crucifixion then becomes part of its meaning (Luke 24: 3-32). It is at this moment that the stranger joins in a meal with the disciples, a meal that is also full of reminiscences of earlier moments; for example, the Last Supper (in which Jesus announced his self-sacrifice and symbolized it in the bread and wine). That meal appears in retrospect to foreshadow later meals in the Christian community that are clearly sacrificial in meaning. The meal enacts the relation between the self-sacrificial purpose of the one who was crucified and the prophetic purposes already shared by the disciples; indeed, the meal later becomes a re-enactment of the initial self-sacrifice – later, but only when the next threshold is crossed in the direction of constructing the complete act.

If the preceding threshold involves primarily language in uniting purpose with meaning, the third threshold bridges the gap between action and response. By action at this stage I mean a composite of will and meaning communicated in word, gesture and deed by all relevant parties. Response, of course, is not necessarily compatible with an action's meaning; it is simply adequate as a signal that the initial action has been taken seriously. To continue answering Peirce's question of how a self-sacrificing action is construed as an act of self-sacrifice, I would suggest that the development of the sacramental meal from the Lord's Supper suggests part of the answer. The statement "Do this in remembrance of me" is quite literally taken up by those who make a memorial out of a meal. The initial action becomes certified as an act of self-sacrifice by those who make the appropriate response in gesture, word, and deed. As a later rite put it, "they offer themselves, their souls and bodies, to be a reasonable, holy, and living sacrifice." Austin (1982) speaks of "uptake" as the response without which a speech-act is not a complete act of speech. Unless a promise is taken seriously as a *bona fide* promise, no promise has really been made. It is the same way with words and gestures that accompany a self-sacrificing action: unless they are taken seriously and issue in the appropriate response, the self-sacrificing action is not being received and certified, so to speak, by the respondents as an act of self-sacrifice directed toward themselves. One can refuse to be self-sacrificing in return or one can join in the action; either way, the initial action becomes a more complete act of self-sacrifice as others respond to it as such.

It is always possible, of course, for none of the intended benefici-aries to respond in complementary ways to an action; cases of extreme alienation do exist in which none of an actor's words, gestures, or deeds receives a complementary response. Action may be coded in ways that are indecipherable by those who would otherwise respond; cases of severe mental illness pose precisely such a problem for the therapist. The respondent may be unable to decipher messages that are a complex mixture of word, gesture, and deed; cases of mental illness may therefore result from such an incapacity as individuals find themselves in an alien social universe and respond in alienated ways. On the other hand, there may be no problems whatsoever in encoding or deciphering such actions and their accompanying words or gestures; individuals do ignore, deny, or reject other individuals. Self-sacrificing actions may therefore perish for lack of complementary interaction long before they are recognized or certified as acts of self-sacrifice. That is why there is some consternation in the New Testament over the individuals who died before the crucifixion or who after the crucifixion remain wholly uninformed and uninterested; they pose a threat to the completion of the act. A significant measure of New Testament theology, as of religious myth generally, as I have already mentioned, is an attempt to account for the deficiencies in acts that would otherwise be perfected.

Theology has no monopoly on the science of completing imperfect acts. What has become known in sociological circles as "symbolic interactionism" is a medley of theses related to the problems of inadequate action and response. On the one hand, action may involve a complex of motives that are only partly framed as intentions, and the intentions may be only partly comprehensible to others in terms of a stated or implied purpose. The actor may also be calling into play a set of roles that are implicit, imaginary, or unconscious, and may take each of those roles more or less seriously. Conversely, those called upon to respond may have a similarly complex set of motives, intentions, and purposes that not only complicate their task of finding meaning in the initial actor's purpose but may lead them to reject or ignore an action whose meaning is entirely clear. The logical possibilities are quite numerous.

Symbolic interactionists may well prefer to see evil and destructive influences as secondary to an order that, left to its own devices, would be intrinsically constructive. Certainly that is why Niebuhr (1949: I, 56–7) gave such very short shrift to Mead in particular. Niebuhr's entire argument assumed that the various sins of unbelief and pride were sources of anxiety and pretension that would inevitably make a perfected act impossible. Here, without reviewing the literature on symbolic interactionism in general and particularly the work of Mead and Cooley, it is sufficient to argue simply that the perfect act remains the holy grail even of this branch of sociology – an ideal from which departures are explained by conflicting definitions of a situation or discrepancies in the extent to which individuals play their roles or take them seriously. The possibility of a wholly adequate response to a well-constructed action remains open, at least in interactionist theory.

The Fragmentation of the Act in Secular Societies

The idea of an act that is complete in every respect, in will and meaning, in its reception and consequences, has been the dream of sociologists, philosophers, saints, and logicians. What are the possibilities of realizing that dream, given the particular characteristics of modern, complex societies and especially the diminishing ability of religion to provide the groundwork for interaction? In a secularizing society the individual's social life no longer provides a spiritual rhetoric by which to recognize human actions as acts of self-sacrifice or spiritual courage. Certainly the mass media and the pop concert can hardly be said to provide a wholesome and coherent expression of human community rooted in profound emotions and spiritual capacities (Wilson 1982: 170). Not even the new religious movements, Wilson argues, provide a sanctuary in which irrational impulses can find expression free from public scrutiny or from the impact of oppressive, rational organization in the new movements themselves (pp. 174–75). The modern wasteland is still a desert. In this book I will be arguing that even the established Churches have lost the authority to define the full range of human motives and actions in terms of sin and salvation. As I have already noted, the rhetoric of confession has become simplified and even confession itself has become merely another liturgical option: hardly a set of words, gestures and deeds that provide consummate actions.

In defining actions as acts, sacred authorities have always permitted the wayward or deviant a certain secrecy of motive and intention; not all actions must be revealed as acts of one kind or another. David Martin's recent work emphasizes that prophetic language, especially in the New Testament, was intended to enlighten only those who have ears to hear (Martin 1980: 121). Like symbols in a dream, religious language, especially in prayer and worship, disguises what is possible in terms of what is familiar and draws "a veil across man's real possibilities" (pp. 124–25); the result is a "cover" for dangerous impulses, motives, and intentions:

> "We are saying that religion, more especially the Christian religion, is one way we imagine limits and potentialities; that it becomes part of the protective cover developed by social structure; that it incorporates a part of that potentiality in order to prevent a devastating explosion."
>
> (Martin 1980: 126)

In a secularizing society the Churches provide less of an expressive mask and Martin's description of a "protective cover" designed to prevent "a devastating explosion" begins to fit a wide range of obsessive, if not wholly neurotic, actions.

The wide availability of religion outside the established Churches of course allows some groups of peoples to adopt sacred masks in publicizing and disguising their political aspirations. Martin quite rightly uses the images of "face," "expression," or "mask" in discussing the symbolic interaction between social movements and central authorities. A religious mask, worn by a group seeking to expand its rights under the law, for instance, enables that group to attract attention or claim legitimacy as well as to remain hidden from too much public scrutiny in an otherwise secular society. Examples abound among contemporary religious sects on both sides of the Atlantic, from the Black Muslims to the Unification Church. The meaning of actions remains problematical when the relevant purposes are covered and disguised by sacred masks.

The mask of protest, however, may be secular when the authority of a nation is based on religious premises, a point that Martin makes especially with regard to the development of a secular political opposition in nineteenth-century France (see Martin 1978b). As modern societies increasingly base their political authority on secular notions of freedom and justice, moreover, the use of religious masks by various dissident groups will undoubtedly spread. It is too soon to argue that religion has been driven from the politics of modern societies; rather, it moves toward the political center from various places on the periphery (see Dobbelaere 1981: 55, Martin 1978b: 77–81). There religion demands to be taken seriously in a public context by the intended beneficiaries of action, where it is still only partially accepted and understood.

One fundamental assertion, made by Martin with especial force, is the starting point for my argument: that religious language is inherently ambiguous and lends itself to many disguises. The prime example, of course, is the *double entendre* of the Kingdom of God, which allows the faithful to claim to be acting out of loyalty to a sovereignty higher than the state, although that action is intrinsically subversive (see Martin 1980: 127 ff.). I would argue, however, that in adopting religious language any social organization or ethnic community takes the risk that its actions will be misunderstood or ignored by the public if not overtly rejected. To offset this risk, those who employ themselves as guardians of sacred mysteries may lay claim to a universal mission that transcends the time and places of a nation's or community's particular history. Certainly a universalizing thrust appears very clearly in the revised versions of liturgies in most Protestant denominations and in the Catholic Church.

In the process of restoring the universal pole to the meaning of such terms as "Kingdom," however, the Churches have ignored or suppressed the rich associations of religious language with the particular experience of historical communities. Religious language, in becoming more universal, also becomes more abstract; in becoming more abstract, it becomes more uniform and general. In the absence of the rich, local fillings that give depth and meaning to religious language, the theological shell becomes simply that – a cover that protects nothing, since there is no local, communal life to shield and to preserve from external scrutiny. Religious language thus comes to represent only the agreed-upon wording of an international religious organization with a few appropriate regional variations. As the church ceases to be a metaphor for the nation and loses its local context, the church also loses its authority to define civic actions in religious terms as acts of self-sacrifice or faithlessness.

Of course, there are too many variations in formal religious practice in modern societies to reduce to a single thesis. Dobbelaere makes it clear that even among major religious organizations there is considerable variation in their approaches to the modern world; Dutch Catholicism, he notes (1981: 121ff.), has adopted a more decentralized and pastoral approach to the transformation of society that allows the Church to be more supportive, less didactic, and less doctrinally remote from everyday life. A fully adequate description of the religious "covers" in modern societies would undoubtedly require attention to new esoteric, therapeutic, and cultic movements as well as to adaptations on the part of dominant religious organizations – a task that Dobbelaere undertakes with suitable caution (pp. 112–16). Nonetheless, I am arguing that religious authority, in becoming more secularized, loses its capacity to define or transform a wide range of actions into acts that have a place in the lexicon, so to speak, of religious pronouncements.

In the next chapter I will discuss the fourth threshold that actions must cross before I would consider them "complete" as acts; here, however, I want to point out once again how hypothetical my notion of a complete act really is. It is hypothetical because it goes beyond any existing construction of actions into acts according to legal or moral criteria; nonetheless, for reasons I will go into shortly, I find it necessary to cite the hypothetical case in order to develop an adequate account of the role of religion in secular societies. It is particularly difficult, under modern conditions, for any actions to be successfully and permanently construed as acts; each of the three thresholds we have so far examined is difficult enough to cross, and the fourth one I am about to consider is even more so. Furthermore, religion is no more able than many other modern institutions to facilitate or guarantee the construction of actions into acts; indeed, ritual in particular, I will argue, reproduces some of the features of modern societies that make all acts problematical. Under these conditions it is difficult to point to any actions that are complete acts in the hypothetical sense of the term that I have adopted here. Why then compound the difficulties of analyzing modern societies by introducing so hypothetical a notion?

Durkheim himself would not approve of my method. On the contrary, he argues that:

> "Now, at the very beginning of research, when the facts have not yet been analyzed, the only ascertainable characteristics are those external enough to be immediately perceived. Those that are less obvious may be perhaps more significant ... [but] they can be anticipated only by substituting some hypothetical conception in place of reality."
>
> (Durkheim 1938: 35)

These "ascertainable" or "external" characteristics are, in Durkheim's views, social facts as obvious as the law and as constraining, say, as the punishments meted out in court. What Durkheim considers obvious and constraining, however, are in modern societies often ambiguous: especially so in cases involving religious belief, practice, and institutions. Individuals engaged in actions that are, in their view, self-sacrificing, are often indicted, tried, and sentenced for crimes such as destroying government property or for contempt of court (Fenn 1982). Durkheim, however, would classify these acts with others that may be less controversial but that also involve criminal citations as a particular case of acts defined, in part, by "the external characteristic that they evoke from society the particular reaction called punishment" (Durkheim 1938: 35); in short, as crimes. Furthermore, what guarantees that these acts are social facts is that the basis for their classification "is to be found in each part because it exists in the whole, rather than in the whole because it exists in the part" (p. 9). The punishment for the crime is simply the way the social fact "expresses itself externally" (p. 10). Why, following Durkheim, would I try to make obscure and hypothetical a base and type of classification (of actions into acts) that Durkheim finds, at least at the beginning of research, to be unproblematical? I have one major reason.

Durkheim appears to believe that the threshold which individual actions cross over on their way to being construed as acts is clear; I disagree. Neither in the construction of motives and intentions, of purposes and meanings, nor of appropriate response to specific actions, is that boundary clear. I am going on to argue, moreover, that many of the more intractable problems encountered by modern societies in construing actions into acts lie precisely in the area that Durkheim considers to be a relatively firm ground for initial research: the process by which actions become fashioned into cases of specific classes or categories of acts. Whether these acts are moral or spiritual, legal or political, the fourth threshold concerns the relation of individual to societal ways of classifying action. Given the high levels of adjudication in modern societies, the frequency of appeals, and widespread dissatisfaction with the results of adjudication, it is "obvious" that the process of constructing actions into acts is problematic in the legal system. The same ambiguities have affected moral judgments, in which the same actions may alternatively be classified in religious, ethical, or therapeutic terms with quite different consequences both for the individuals directly affected and for the society as a whole. There is no agreement, for instance, on whether actions that may appear self-sacrificial (e.g. in civil disobedience) are illegal, immoral, religious, self-serving, or even symptomatic of mental or emotional pathology. Whether the process of construing these actions into acts is formal or informal, and whether the relevant courts belong to the state, the federal government, or to the "court" of public opinion, the final threshold is not easily crossed.

The threshold or boundary separating individual actions from acts that are recognizable as social facts is apparently like a membrane that is permeable in both directions; across this membrane pass influences from the individual to the society and in the opposite direction. The flow of influences is continuous, reversible in direction, and may have either beneficial or destructive consequences. That is why sociologists have been particularly interested in what has become known as "labeling theory": a set of ideas which attempts to give a complete account of the process by which actions become recognized, certified, or judged as acts. Conversely, labeling theory also accounts for a process by which new categories (e.g. of criminality) are first constructed, with the result that actions formally considered neutral or ambiguous become potentially illegal. Labeling theory is particularly interested, furthermore, in accounting for the role of third parties (e.g. the press) in the process by which politicians or the courts construe certain actions as acts. While its critics consider it pretentious to call labeling theory a "theory," its difficulties attest to the complexity of accounting for the process by which social systems and individuals manufacture actions into acts. As with any process of manufacturing, where ownership is separate from control and production is geared to the needs of a distant or hypothetical market, the manufacture of actions into acts is highly complex, and the products are quickly obsolescent.

Whereas religion in simpler societies may have fostered the completion of actions into acts within the channels of legal or political authority or through the operation of the less formal constraints and pressures of public opinion, a secular society has made it far more difficult for religion, whether institutional or popular, to assist in the manufacture of actions into acts. The process of secularization has drastically reduced the scope of the Churches' authority to assess and award civil damages, dispense from a treasury of social merit, and make up for social inequities. These ways of exercising authority now are the prerogative of institutions outside clerical control. Certainly the Churches have long since forfeited their ability to preside over the assessing and awarding of claims to various damages and now enter courts as parties to litigation – a considerable loss of authority. Despite the continuing emphasis on religion in education long after the British Industrial Revolution, the Churches have even lost control over the educational system (Dobbelaere 1981: 70). Even in Belgium, where the Catholic Church actively defended its educational institutions from outside control, Dobbelaere notes that the Church faces pedagogical criticism, and doctors and social workers have successfully imposed their professional standards and policies on the Church's hospitals and welfare organizations (pp. 67–68). In Holland the Dutch Catholics similarly have even lost exclusive control over their own educational and medical institutions as doctors and teachers have come to set the standards for professional activity (p. 68). In counting up sins and in dispensing merit the professions have the upper hand.

The Church has suffered a comparable loss of ability to shield an individual from public scrutiny and so to confine sin to a privileged area of private life. Where the Church once defined the precincts of the sacred and afforded protection to the sinner, secular professions now define the boundaries of the private sphere. Of course, the Church does not yield its authority completely. Dobbelaere remarks that the Catholic Church in Belgium still seeks to regulate the private life of individuals who teach in Catholic schools, despite the lay teachers' resistance to ecclesiastical control (p. 69). In Catholic hospitals, however, lay practitioners have succeeded in defining the private sphere in ways which drastically limit the authority and relevance of Catholic teaching; religion now concerns the purely personal and interpersonal, whereas doctors make the critical decisions regarding medical practice in such sensitive areas as sterilization and abortion, and professionalized managers and administrators determine the routines of hospital administration (see Dobbelaere 1981: 78–79). Therefore the distinction between what is private and what is public has become both problematical and political. Because it is problematical, Dobbelaere warns us, the criteria of the public marketplace (efficiency, for instance, and rationality) may invade the privacy of the family or of friendship. Because it is political, the Church must enter the lists in opposition to other interested parties who have now joined the effort to draw the boundary between the public and private spheres of social life (p. 84). Sociologists are left to wonder where the private sphere is to be found rather than to take uncritically the notion that such a sphere enjoys clear, let alone sacred, boundaries. As Dobbelaere points out, "the use of the terms 'private' and 'public' should be the *object* of sociological inquiry, since these notions are social definitions and not sociological categories" (p. 84). I wholly agree.

Awards of credit, like punishment for wrong-doing, increasingly belong to the organizations that give degrees, license professionals, enforce the law, and provide for punishments and damages when offense is given or taken. To institutionalize freedom as a way of life may have required the Protestant Reformation; certainly Parsons (1963) is right in giving Protestantism credit for making individual responsibility a central value in Western societies. I agree with Parsons that denominations were a result of Protestantism, an on-going expression of Protestantism's trust in the individual, and a further stimulus to individuals to take responsibility for their own beliefs. Others have more recently argued a similar point: that the middle classes in England spread their influence and acquired power to the extent that they took responsibility for the controlled expres-sion of motives and intentions in every aspect of their lives (see Carroll 1981: 491–93). To lose the protection of the Church and to become free of the hidden forces that disturb the soul has certainly diminished the authority of official religion and the appeal of magic while making the individual increasingly responsible for his or her own salvation. I will argue later that along with responsibility, guilt has become covert and operates as an inarticulate premise or way of life; it is guilt, however, without absolution and release save in occasional amnesties.

It is unnecessary to review all the relevant sociological opinion on the form and function of guilt, and in any event Dobbelaere has covered this issue quite fairly indeed. He notes, for instance, that Bellah characterizes the religious culture of modern societies as offer-ing no "personal escape from social and political exigencies, but rather a stress on inner authenticity and autonomy, which has pro-found social and moral consequences" (Dobbelaere 1981: 100). Dobbelaere notes that this responsibility for one's own salvation can be profoundly unsettling but that Bellah does not deal with this burden of guilt (p. 100). Dobbelaere's discussion underlines how limited a contribution formal religion can make in relieving the very burden of guilt for which it bears some historical responsibility.

In the process of secularization individuals become increasingly aware of their obligations to themselves and to others, but those obligations may be increasingly limited. That is the clear argu-ment behind Parsons's evolutionary scheme for interpreting modern societies. Each institution elaborates its own rules in a pattern that is consistent with the most general values of the society as a whole, and those values, in turn, require that the individual take on the responsibility for working out his or her salvation in each institutional sphere. The private sphere becomes one in which the individual can be trusted to be working on salvation in a way that is at least not inconsistent with the values of the larger society. On the other hand, Luckmann (1967) and Herberg (1967) argue that the existential solutions of individuals to the problem of defining and justifying their own existence may be at some variance with the operating or effective values of the larger society; consistency is a value but not a fact of modern societies (see Dobbelaere 1981: 96–103). In that connection I will argue in this book that the Churches are leaving individuals to work out the specific terms of their own salvation without providing a discourse capable of assessing guilt and providing absolution. To that extent, the Churches are killing the dream of the completed and wholly sufficient act.

2

The Fourth Threshold:
Binding the Individual
and Society in One Act

At the fourth threshold, I suggest, there are *two* types of rationality that need to be served. On the one hand, there is the reasoning of the individual who is taking the action: mailing a letter, voting in an election, prophesying, or even predicting. On the other hand, there is the reason of the social system: system rationality, for lack of a better term. To mail a letter requires that one satisfy at least minimally the standards of the post office for postage, for depositing mail, and for addressing the envelope; the electoral system has a similar set of requirements that are rational in terms of the system itself. Neither system's rationality regards the individual's intention or purpose in writing a letter or voting. When the action of voting is finally classified as an act, its meaning to the system (as a "mandate" for a party or a reaffirmation of trust in the democratic system) will also follow a logic quite independent of the individual's own action; it is easy for a vote made in protest to be considered part of a mandate, or for a vote withheld to be taken, not as a sign of protest, but of trust in the system. The classification of such actions as acts will no doubt be affected by the way a system is ordered: its specific provisions for mailing or voting, but also its rules, explanations, and its general justifications. At the final threshold of action, then, there are two types of rationality; for lack of better terms, I will call them personal rationality and systemic rationality.

At least in theory, it is always possible for the two types of rationality to be joined harmoniously. Hobbes, after imagining social life as a war of all against all, in which force and fraud become necessary if individuals are to secure their own means and reach their several ends, posited the state as a solution to this conflict; in speaking of Hobbes's solution, Parsons (1949) wrote:

> "This solution really involves stretching, at a critical point, the conception of rationality beyond its scope in the rest of the theory, to the point where the actors come to realise the situation as a whole instead of pursuing their own ends in terms of their immediate situation, and then take the action necessary to eliminate force and fraud, and, purchasing security at the sacrifice of the advantages to be gained by their future employment. This is not the solution in which the present study will be interested."
>
> (In Mayhew 1982: 100)

It *is* part of the solution, however, in which I am interested. In this solution, what makes sense to the individual is only attainable in compliance with a system that deprives all of the citizens of some of their wishes. There is an order here in which desired actions become desirable among all those whose survival or well-being depends on the maintenance of that system. Otherwise their actions will pursue ends that are entirely personal – ends which are "random" only so far as the system is concerned, and which, to be reached, require a certain inequality in the amount of hope which is distributed to individuals and to social classes. For Hobbes, a certain "equality of hope" avoids a situation in which force and fraud become reasonable; it is more advantageous to perpetuate such a system than the war of all against all (see O'Neill 1976). The alternative is stark, in which life is more solitary, poor, brutish, and nasty for some than for others, but for all may be relatively short.

Here I am arguing that there can be a rationality that transcends the split between personal and systemic rationality that I have already mentioned. As I have mentioned, to Parsons this is of course "stretching, at a critical point, the conception of rationality," but I prefer to think that Parsons and perhaps sociologists in general have too limited a notion of rationality. It is customary for sociologists to write as if either the social system or the individual are rational but not both; for them both to achieve a common rationality is a possibility far too utopian for the sociologist used to dichotomies like "individual and society" or "formal versus substantive rationality." Social life is too easily split, in sociological thinking, between values that are "sentimental" and therefore appealing to individuals and values that are "rational" because they make sense of the division of labor in a society (see O'Neill 1976). I posit no such inevitable dichotomy here; at the fourth threshold an action can indeed be completed by incorporating the action of the individual within the categories of a social system; otherwise a deed is destined to be merely a random action lost in a chaotic or at least partially framed social environment. The possibility of an act becoming complete depends, of course, on the three "thresholds" or conditions which I covered in the first chapter. The fourth, however, raises a question concerning principles of order, and it is that question which this chapter will address.

Sociology has tended to assume that either a system has rationality or that persons are rational – but not both. This is hardly the point at which to try to summarize a complex body of social theory; the summary by O'Neill (1976), to which I have referred, is more than adequate. Here I would only point out the logic that such theory adopts. If, for instance, one assumes that individuals taken as a category are irrational, one looks to a social system to supply the missing voice of reason. If, to be more specific, one assumes that for the mass of individuals ends are random, only the social system will necessarily supply a measure of simplicity and unification of the ends of action. In the same vein, if one assumes that individuals as a whole are interested only in exploiting one another in pursuit of their separate satisfactions, one will seek to find in a social system the requisite control against exploitative action and the rewards for cooperation; Hobbes's "solution" is a prime example. Finally, to assume that individuals are generically capable only of a technical sort of rationality that focuses on means and forgets ends, no doubt one will find in a social system the missing repository of values. Call this "type A" sociological thinking, that posits system rationality as an antidote to the irrationality of individuals *per se*.

There are many examples of such thinking, either among the writings of Emile Durkheim or, for that matter, among current critics of individualism in American society. The recent collection of studies of individuals by associates of Bellah (1985) intends to illustrate the incapacity of individuals to stretch their rationality beyond the immediate, the practical, and the concrete. We are familiar with the theory behind such a description; it forms the core of Durkheim's attack on the pragmatists, as I noted in the Introduction. No one would be surprised, therefore, to find individuals criticized in these studies for their own pragmatic approaches to the dilemmas of social life and for their failure to see the extent to which their individual lives are grounded in and can only be fulfilled by the society in which they live. The same authors also may be too despairing of modern societies to argue that the United States can offer the completion of individual actions into enduring and valuable social acts; that is quite another matter. Certainly they agree with Parsons that it is stretching the concept of rationality to think that individuals as we now know them in a society like the contemporary United States could "come to realize the situation as a whole instead of pursuing their own ends in terms of their immediate situation" (Parsons in Mayhew 1982: 100). In sociological thinking of this type (A), only the society as a whole can offer values and ends that are sufficiently general and appealing to transcend the utilitarian and restricted aspects of personal rationality; it is simply too bad that modern societies have forgotten their inheritance of collective sentiments and are so unable to supply the missing transcendence.

In one respect there is in Western religion a pious expression of this viewpoint. In the rites (revised or otherwise) of most Christian churches, there is a combination of collect and confession that expresses precisely this notion of the origin of evil in individualistic strivings and limitations. It is individuals who have "followed too much the devices and desires of their own hearts"; it is only in the gathering of the faithful that their separate ends may be collected into a single voice that has reason and that transcends and fulfills each person's private ends. That is indeed the function of the prayer-form known as the "collect": to collect these separate and random ends into one. No doubt there are other, perhaps better examples of this aspect of religious institutions; certainly this example is incomplete, since it ignores for the moment the context of such piety or the scope of the institution itself. More on that later, of course. Here I am simply pointing to a parallel in religious thought for the sociological understanding of evil as originating in the private pursuit of personal rationality. The question is whether it is merely utopian to think of a rationality that integrates the ends of the person with those of a social system without sacrificing either meaningful freedom or a social order that offers an "equality," so to speak, "of hope" (see O'Neill 1976).

It is the tendency of sociological theory to think in terms of dichotomies, I am suggesting, that makes the unification of personal rationality and systemic rationality seem utopian. Take, for our second example, a type (B) of sociological thought that finds social systems rather than individuals lacking in rationality. On this view the possibility of completing actions into acts is just as dismal as it is when individuals are lacking in rationality and social systems alone provide principles of order. In the light of this second sociological viewpoint, however, individuals will be disappointed in seeking to complete their actions into acts because the system itself is anarchic, confusing, unfair, and exploitative. Since the economy, for instance, is anarchic (and it may be), it is up to individuals and groups to organize their work along lines that are less individualistic and more fraternal, less competitive and more cooperative. On this view, since the social system operates on a purely formal rationality and so emphasizes its rules and procedures regardless of the needs of particular individuals in specific situations, it is up to individuals to introduce a more "substantive" rationality into their social life, to demand participation and fairness, and to insist on work and politics as vehicles for creative self-expression.

In overcoming the irrationality of a society, individuals may join affinity groups or unions, and the chaos of the marketplace may be overcome to the extent that individuals form cartels or restrict their economic activities to what can be traded locally and made in a commune of fraternal workers. In the same way, to overcome the irrationality of a society that places its own principles of organization ahead of what makes sense to or satisfies individuals, it may be necessary to form associations of welfare recipients or of tenants and even at times to interrupt the smooth activities of the Dean's office or of the Board of Trustees. The ways of association and participation are not always smooth in a social system that is short on systemic rationality. For one type of viewpoint, it is rationality in the system that is lacking; for the other, it is individuals themselves who – as individuals – cannot order or frame their actions. They agree that because of a splitting-off of rationality between individuals and systems, actions will always be incomplete as fully constituted acts. It is this pessimism that I am challenging here.

I have already outlined some of the conditions that will have to be satisfied before an action can be fully rational in both the personal and systemic senses of that term. The four thresholds range from the most intimate social context to the most distant, and from the simplest to the most complicated dimensions of social action. Certainly it is not only a religious dream that a person's motives and intentions be integrated and communicated in acts of will. It is also a widely shared aspiration for personal authenticity that motives (e.g. self-hatred or revenge) not be disguised as an intention to sacrifice the self. The combination of motive and intention becomes a will that, at the second threshold, may be expressed in terms of various purposes that are relevant to others in the individual's most immediate range of social action; these purposes, however, may conflict with others' designs. To define their relationship may require additional voices from other social contexts or generations. I will take up this possibility in Chapter 4. Certainly religion has no monopoly on aspirations for meaningful as well as authentic action, nor is it utopian to believe that action can become meaningful to others who have disparate or even conflicting purposes; Jesus's symbolic action in the Last Supper is a case in point, in which he framed his purpose in meanings that were derived from ecclesiastical, prophetic, and eschatological traditions in the Jewish community. The third threshold to be crossed requires others to respond seriously to an action, others who were not present at its inception and who might well come from other locales, communities, and generations: the public, in short, for whom the action must acquire significance. The New Testament was written partly in an effort to establish what a proper response would be and who would be allowed or required to make it. Here the range of social action involves the possibility of actors coming from contexts that were not represented in the initial circumstances: from non-believers, perhaps, and even those who were not members of the Jewish community. Finally, as significant response is framed to incorporate significant action, the fourth threshold is approached: call it macro-social, for lack of a better word. The first thresholds involved the relation of the individual to other individuals, present or absent, part of the same community or generation or coming from quite different times and places; still, these are individuals or groups of individuals and not representatives or agents of a society or social system as a whole. The fourth threshold, to be crossed, requires that such action, fully framed in intention, meaning, and significant response, be completed by the larger society and its major institutions where its effects will ramify throughout a whole social system. Thus an act of self-sacrifice becomes an act of blasphemy to the Jewish nation and, to the Roman

Empire, treason. Its effects are macro-social, whether or not they are positive or negative.

While it is not too utopian to imagine a society that integrates personal with systemic rationality, the question remains, "under what conditions is it possible for individuals and societies to synthesize the two types of rationality?" To put it more simply, societies are to varying degrees pathological, since they split off one type of reasoning from the other. Sociology is in fact one discipline that diagnoses and recommends remedies for social pathology. From the point of view of managing a social system, it may make sense for sociologists to advocate bussing students out of their neighborhoods to public schools; the public response is a matter of record and documents the wide gap between the principles by which individuals or groups act and those that may enhance the effectiveness of the social system. Sociologists are better at diagnosing than at prescribing; perhaps that is inevitable, since any action in a system that splits off one type of rationality from another is bound to have unintended and unhappy consequences. Individuals may have their rationality ignored by the system or achieve their rationality despite the resistance or chaos of the system itself; either pattern is, sociologically speaking, pathological.

It is not too utopian to anticipate a form of society in which actions are completed into acts that are rational in both the personal and systemic sense so long as it is possible for societies not only to have the same spiritual problems but to employ the same resources for renewal as individuals. Here I will be asking whether religion itself can be not only a symptom of individual and social pathology but also a vehicle for redemption of both social system and individuals. In the light of the criticism of religion, and especially of Marxist criticism, it is clear that the split in rationality that I have been describing finds expression in religion. Religion may dramatize this splitting of rationality, or religion may seek to disguise it, relieve its symptoms, and prevent its worst consequences. Those possibilities will occupy us later in this book. Here I am considering whether these latter possibilities are not too limited. Indeed, I am suggesting that under certain conditions a society is possible in which actions can be fully completed as acts without loss of either personal or systemic rationality.

The Renewal of the Individual and of Society

One can take a very dim view of the moral and spiritual capacities of social systems like the nation. Niebuhr argued that, whereas individuals could repent themselves and forgive others, "the mind and heart of collective man is notoriously less imaginative than that of the individual" (Niebuhr 1935: 129), a clear example of type B thinking in theological form. Niebuhr "knows" that the only way to heal antagonisms that destroy nations and individuals is through "a forgiving love, grounded in repentance," but he also "knows" that "that degree of love is an impossibility for nations" (pp. 128–29). In a time of preparations for nuclear war it would seem more essential than ever to test the strength of Niebuhr's pessimism against the real possibilities of collective repentance and renewal. In the last ten years there have indeed been some extraordinary gestures of reconciliation across national boundaries. If other such acts do not follow, there may be no alternative to wars that inevitably bring mutual destruction. To repeat Parsons once more, it will then be too late for societies or individuals "to realize the situation as a whole instead of pursuing their own ends in terms of their immediate situation" (in Mayhew 1982: 100).

Of course, Niebuhr may be right that modern societies are caught within an "ineluctable fate" that will lead to their destruction. Modern nations may indeed not know their limits, may fail to take seriously their responsibilities, and may very well destroy themselves and others by trying to take history into their own hands. Certainly in any age it is dangerous for a nation to identify its own interests with the fate of the world. No international community now exists with the strength to check the will-to-power of the largest nations. According to this viewpoint (B), which Niebuhr tends to represent, individuals may very well transform themselves in time through leaps of their imagination. Not so the nation. That social system seems unable to complete actions into acts and so to unite individuals with collective principles of order.

Later, in subsequent chapters, I will argue that, under certain conditions, rituals have enabled action to cross the fourth threshold and so unite personal with systemic forms of rationality. Being a theologian in the prophetic tradition (and not a sociologist), Niebuhr understandably ignores how, in corporate ritual, individuals act collectively; they vow to enable life to go on from one generation to the next, from one stage in life to the next, as individuals' actions are incorporated into collective acts. Just as an individual may resolve something through smashing a pot filled with an ancestor's ashes or by exchanging vows, so a society may break with its past and make new commitments for an otherwise indefinite future in acts that conjoin personal with systemic principles of order.

In modern societies, of course, it is exceedingly difficult to find a ritual, like the rite of enthronement, for instance, in which the reign of a new king inaugurates a period of new hope for a society and perhaps of new vitality for the individual citizen. Durkheim's interest in ritual stemmed from a search for modern analogues to rites which used to renew simpler societies and enthuse their citizenry in ways that benefited the whole rather than dissipated their energies into a wide range of individualistic or trivial pursuits. A modern wedding for the English monarchy or a national football championship match in the United States provides more limited and temporary benefits to portions of a society rather than more enduring benefits to the whole body politic. Niebuhr's focus on prophetic biblical faith, with its fundamental scorn of rituals and solemnities, initially excludes a search in modern rites for forms of renewal that allow an entire community or nation to renew itself with promising words and gestures. Still, I must ask whether there are rites that would perform such a function, and whether the conditions exist in modern societies for them to do so effectively.

Of course, in the larger and more complex nations rituals may no longer provide occasions that move entire communities while mobilizing individual citizens; there are always many missing places at any corporate feast. The invited guests have other interests, and many more who might have attended are uninterested or fail to receive an invitation. To be sure, even on a primitive island a community's rituals have a few empty places, perhaps, and there is grumbling among those sitting in the lower seats at the feast. In a nation as complex as America, however, the rejoicing at major national festivities is universally televised, but not everyone is watching and fewer still are taking part. The inauguration of a President, even a papal visit, leaves no lasting benefit or treasury of merit on which others can later draw for a fresh supply of social credit. Of course, there are ritualistic or ritualized aspects of social life even in a self-declared secular democracy, and I will consider them in later chapters. Here, in focusing on the fourth threshold of action, I am asking whether any rites can transcend the differences between individual and corporate forms and sources of renewal.

The question takes on added significance when we return to the example of self-sacrifice. There are rites (e.g. those of Memorial Day in the United States) which commemorate individual acts of self-sacrifice precisely because they contribute to the continuity and survival of a social system, the nation, which is enjoined to similar actions with a corresponding purpose and dedication. It is not clear, therefore, that the nation *per se*, when compared with groups and communities, is more impervious to correction, less aware of its own limitations, and more inclined to identify the ultimate end of history with its own more limited ends of history.

In this work I am focusing simply on rituals as techniques for completing actions into acts at all four thresholds of action, but I am particularly concerned here, and in conclusion, with the fourth threshold. Can rituals set limits on the ambitions and strivings not only of individuals but of entire social systems, including the modern nation, acting as a safeguard against their own unlimited pretensions?

Where ritual fails to combine personal with systemic forms of rationality, a culture may nevertheless provide the proper limitations to pretension and sacrifice. In the prophetic faith most hostile to ritual, however, there are invitations to a people even to sacrifice national security rather than to temporize with enemies of the faith – a Jonestown mentality, one might say. Of course, when an individual chooses martyrdom, the community remembers and may even be strengthened; it *is* expedient that only one should die instead of a people. But biblical prophecy contains an invitation to martyrdom that could tempt an entire society to risk itself in order to provoke some final judgment by history on the relative merits of that nation's claim to respect, to honour, even, perhaps, to glory. If a nation dreams of a glorious day in which all other nations come to pay it tribute, and if, furthermore, a nation knows that its god will vindicate all those who risk all for their faith, a nation could conclude that one final sacrifice of the body politic, once and for all, could usher in a new era of vindication and even of triumph. It is a dangerous illusion for individuals to entertain – but catastrophic for nations. Ritual may anticipate, partially enact, and postpone the final day of judgment; even ritual may fail, and in modern societies the conditions are ripe for ritual to fail at the critical fourth threshold of action. That leaves the door open for religious culture to stimulate a collective course of action that ritual could both anticipate and prevent.

Niebuhr is very adamant, in his earlier writing, that societies lack the spiritual resources for renewal that can come to individuals through the biblical tradition:

"The collective behavior of mankind is not imaginative enough to assure more than minimal approximations of the ideal [of love]. Genuine forgiveness of the enemy requires a contrite recognition of the sinfulness of the self and of the mutual responsibility for the sin of the accused. Such spiritual penetration is beyond the capacities of collective man."

(Niebuhr 1935: 111)

Such charity presumably is beyond the spiritual "capacities of collective man" because social organizations are themselves incapable of the faith and hope which alone can issue in love. Niebuhr's early writing is uniformly bleak in its portrait of the spiritual capacities of social systems. When he proclaims, for instance, that "the mind and heart of collective man is notoriously less imaginative than that of the individual," any attempts to raise social conflicts to a spiritual level can only "produce a tragic by-product of the spiritual accentuation of natural conflict" (Niebuhr 1935: 127). This is undoubtedly because "parties to a dispute inevitably make themselves judges over it and thus fall into the sin of pretending to be God" (p. 126).

Here I have questioned this despairing prophecy on the spiritual capacities of *all* social systems; although the prophecy clearly and, I believe, rightly condemns the nation-*state*, there may well be conditions in which a social system can renew faith, rekindle hope, and exercise charity. The sociological question asks for the conditions that are more or less conducive to the spiritual regeneration of social systems as a whole. These conditions profoundly affect the ability of certain rituals to express, to enact, and to resolve the grievances that underlie even the smoothest forms of social life.

Of course, few writers are consistently despairing of collective virtues, and Niebuhr is no exception. Although he clearly prefers an individualistic and prophetic form of piety, he occasionally holds out hope for the redemption of a whole social system. Having pointed out that the Church can itself sustain and be sustained by faith, hope, and love, he is forced by the logic of his own example to ask:

"what light this Christian doctrine of the renewal of life throws upon the fate of civilizations and cultures. Can they escape death by rebirth? Is the renewal or rebirth of individual life an analogy for the possibilities of man's collective enterprises?"

(Niebuhr 1949: 215)

After all, Niebuhr had argued that, "when followed consistently, the biblical faith must be fruitful of genuine renewals of life in history, *in both the individual and collective existence of man*" (p. 215; emphasis added). Niebuhr himself is not consistent on this point, but the burden of his argument certainly casts perennial doubt on the possibility of any collective transformations except under biblical auspices.

3

The First Threshold: Will, Motive, and Intention

When Kierkegaard argued that "purity of heart is to will one thing," he wrote the book, so to speak, on how difficult it is to cross even the first threshold toward a single, complete act. In that crossing, motives are expressed in intentions, no doubt, but these intentions may or may not be consistent with the motives themselves. The proverbial pavement on the road to hell leads in the direction of torment precisely because, beneath that pavement or covering, lie hidden the motives that belie good intentions. To will one thing, then, is to be single-minded: to have a mind in which conscious intentions derive directly from and do not disguise motives that are often hardly conscious. In this chapter I will be talking about the difficulties that attend the fusing of motive and intention into will: the first threshold of action. Toward the end of this chapter I will take up again the question of how a ritual may enable that first passage to take place.

It is not surprising that religion should provide both a remedy in ritual for the divided mind and a diagnosis of those divisions. Here I will use the concept of sin as one example of religion's diagnosis and treatment of the division between motive and intention; that is all I can seek to accomplish on that subject here. The literature on the concept has been accumulating for nearly two millennia, and even a brief synopsis of the history of the concept, besides being beyond my own competence, would pre-empt my main purpose. That purpose is to develop a sociological account of the attempt to complete action into acts: an account that depends heavily on theological and psychoanalytic understandings and yet remains within a sociological framework for the study of action in complex social systems like the modern nation-state.

Impediments to Crossing the First Threshold: Anxiety

Perhaps the primary sign of a split between motive and intention is anxiety. By this I do not mean simply to point out how anxiety betrays the destructive impulse hiding behind an apparently benign action; of course, that betrayal is relevant and I will return to it later. Here I mean by anxiety something more basic: anxiety at being in the world, at being helpless and alone, at being separated from or abandoned by those on whom one's life depends. Even more basic, of course, is the initial panic at being born. Here is one account of the relation of that primal anxiety to more adult worries and fear:

> "In his explanation Freud assumed that birth was the prototypical situation of anxiety, a point at which the organism is flooded with stimuli over which it can exercise no control. However, in the maturation process, and by learning as a function of experience, this automatic, involuntary anxiety is transformed: a crucial transition occurs, from the automatic experience of anxiety to the intentional reproduction of anxiety as a signal of danger."
>
> (Weinstein and Platt 1973: 35)

This statement, coming from an excellent essay on the relation of psychoanalytic to sociological theory, has overtones of the pragmatist outlook which sociology itself initially attacked; other sources to which I will turn for additional psychoanalytic insight are more consistent with the position of Durkheim that I outlined in the Introduction. Here it is enough, however, to note the critical distinction between motive and intention: anxiety as a mature (i.e. intentional) response to realistic perceptions of potential loss or danger, and anxiety as the (motivated) panic of the new born. Anxiety is therefore the *sign* of a disjunction between motive and intention.

Anxiety as a sign of a divided mind may indicate the presence of the type of panic these authors mention: the panic of a newborn self overwhelmed by a world in which it feels lost. The attempt to cover, conceal, control, and overcome such anxiety may lead even the relatively mature adult to seek to master the "world" by reason, by ideological efforts at oversimplification and control, or by religious systems that order and integrate human experience within a cosmic framework. Less abstract or intellectual efforts may lead the mature adult to order the world in a way which allows one to grasp or enter in: very much as a newborn seeks to grasp the mother or even in fantasy to enter once again the closed circumference of the womb. Any social context can provide such an occasion for apparently mature intentions that nonetheless express and also conceal the most primitive anxiety. Here I use "anxiety" simply as a sign that the motives of an action may exceed or belie the intent to grasp or have access to some social world in ways that at least *appear* normal, reasonable, or adult.

Here my use of "anxiety" resembles, at least superficially, one theological conception of anxiety as being, in itself, the primary sin. Niebuhr has argued that anxiety is a sin because it derives from an even more primary source: the sin of unbelief. Anxiety over being helpless and alone, in the world with powers on which one depends but over which one has no control, reflects the absence of belief and therefore becomes sinful. Later forms of sin derive from the initial unbelief and its consequent anxiety: the sin of self-deception which, according to Niebuhr (1953: I, 203–07), is an attempt to fool others as well as ourselves concerning one's true importance. In the absence of belief, the self experiences itself as fragile indeed and hardly worth the attention or the claims made for oneself; the collusion of others, Niebuhr notes, and a preoccupation with the affairs of everyday life are not sufficient to allay the underlying sense of worthlessness that only faith can relieve. It is in this interplay between the basic motive, to guarantee the continuation or worth of the self, and the intention, which may have a wide range of practical or moral expressions, that anxiety arises and expresses the presence of an underlying split between the two levels of consciousness.

The psychoanalytic literature is quite clear on the subject of individuals whose intentions are adult but whose motives are rooted in an earlier stage of life with its particular dangers, fears, and adaptations; regression is the source of this split between levels of conscious motivation. Weinstein and Platt summarize the position this way:

> "The gradual ability to distinguish present (actual) danger from potential danger, and situations of danger from traumatic situations, is a measure of the maturity of reality testing; failure to make such distinctions is a sign of regression."
>
> (Weinstein and Platt 1973: 36)

Set aside for the moment questions about the notion of "reality" embedded in the concept of reality-testing; as I have mentioned, these authors remind us of the initial polemic of Durkheim's (1955) sociology against pragmatism. What matters is the authors' summation of the notion of regression as a failure of the individual to lay to rest motives that may have been essential to survival in situations in which, as a young human being, the individual is vulnerable and in danger. Those motives can be the source of a backward pull on even the most adult intentions to cope with the world in terms of real rather than exaggerated or imagined dangers.

Take, for example, the constant reminder by Jews and Christians of periods in which their ancestors indeed suffered and died in ways that still frighten the imagination. The reminders of their subjugation in Egypt or at the hands of the Romans, of their perilous crossings from death to life, keep alive memories of suffering that was indeed traumatic if not also fatal. The allusions to the parting of the waters of the Red Sea and a participation through baptism and a spiritual birth in the death and resurrection of Christ suggest that the panic evoked by these collective memories is intended to express the panic of the newborn in a world overwhelming and out of control. The reiteration of these memories in the context of a ritual is no doubt intended to inspire new faith; I will take up the question of baptism in this connection rather shortly. Here I am pointing out that the same adult purpose may cover a regressive tendency to code present and potential dangers as potentially traumatic. Religion, in other words, may perpetuate and express the tension between early motive and later intention that it also seeks to transcend; trying to inspire faith, religion may succeed in reinvigorating the early panic of the individual at the moment of birth and rekindle memories of early trauma in the history of a society. Religion intensifies the memory and strengthens the imagination in ways that may give the lie to its stated intention of making the world a better place.

Impediments to Crossing the First Threshold: Fantasy and "the World"

If the first impediment is a mind divided between motive and intention, the second is a mind that is prematurely "made up." I use the phrase "made up" because of its connotations; something made-up is fabricated, perhaps fictitious, as well as set in a certain direction.

"Make-up" is cosmetic; and yet to "make up" with someone is to reconcile differences. It is in this sense of a contrived reconciliation of parts of the mind that I speak of a mind that is "made up"; it has covered the difference between motive and intention well enough to present its face to the world.

An intention is therefore a way of approaching the world out there, in ways which may have as much to do with partially conscious or wholly unconscious motives as with conscious intent. The mind, having constructed elements of motive and intention into an orientation toward the world, may have certain aspects of the world uppermost in mind. Using a sociological (Parsonian) scheme for listing such orientations, one psychoanalyst notes that the individual may have several intentions: to adapt to the world as a set of "exigencies" and constraints or to attain certain goals by using parts of the world or consuming them; alternatively, the individual may be oriented toward the world less with interests in mind than a search for standards by which to make choices or for values by which to make existential commitments (Edelson 1976: 160 ff.). Edelson's use of Parsons's scheme is highly tentative and selective, however, because Parsons himself left a confusing record of his own interpretations of his action schema: at times the scheme related more to the intentions and motives of the ego, but earlier interpretations derived from Parsons's understanding of the id. There is indeed a switch in Parsons, which Edelson notes, from his earlier work on action to his theories on how social systems cohere (see Edelson 1976: 160 ff.). Edelson's point is worth making again here: that the combination of motive and intention places the individual in an orientation toward the world that is really an imaginative construction of the self and the world. Although some psychoanalysts still insist that "illness is equivalent to subjugation to fantasy, to the nonrational, while health is equivalent to recognition of brute reality," Edelson argues against the "often unwitting assumption . . . that there is one true reality and that it is possible to know it directly, independently of any imaginative apprehension of it or valuation of it" (Edelson 1976: 159).

My preference for Edelson's viewpoint finds support in the sociological polemic against pragmatism. In the Introduction I cited Durkheim's (1955) criticism of pragmatism for failing to distinguish the question of reality from the truth question; here it is Edelson who raps the knuckles of those who think of "one true reality" as though reality were inseparable from truth. Like Durkheim, Edelson is aware that the social world is a mental construction, just as the mind includes contents that can be derived only from social and cultural life: images, symbols, identifications, prohibitions, sanctions, and memories of others' experience. Edelson places the imagination and its work through dream and fantasy at a central place in explaining orientations that owe at least as much to society and to the mind itself as they do to the drives of the organism for security, pleasure, and survival (see Lifton 1976: 49 ff.).

This viewpoint is sharply opposed to pragmatist notions of human development and adaptation. Weinstein and Platt, in their own attempt to synthesize sociological and psychoanalytic theory, argue for sharper distinctions between the self and society (Weinstein and Platt 1973). On the one hand, the social world is not a mere extension of the family or a projection of the individual's early experience; according to Weinstein and Platt, it has its own, hard reality and has a determining role in the individual's mental life from the pre-Oedipal phase onward (pp. 58–9). Society is like the "environment" in pragmatist thought. Conversely, whether a "society approves or not," individuals may not cherish or revere a society's "standards and expectations" and may redefine them rather liberally (p. 72). Edelson, on the contrary, dislikes the assumption "of a something 'out there' that exists independently of the subjective activity of the mind that knows it, a something that is in and of itself indifferent to the wishes, desires, intentions, anticipations or orientations to future end-states, attitudes, preferences, or values and interests constituting such activity" (Edelson 1976: 159). The "world" as such, then, is a psychic reality; its truth is another question, and it is one to which religion is pre-eminently addressed.

Much of what may seem extreme in Edelson's argument really embodies that Durkheimian logic that simultaneously stresses opposing but not contradictory aspects of social life: its psychic nature on the one hand, and its rootedness in what is external and prior to any specific individual. Taking the generic individual as a starting point, it is clear that social life is a construction of individual mind; thought and imagination, intention and motive are the mental bases from which individuals together construct laws, found institutions, declare war, make sacraments, inaugurate regimes, and so on. On the other hand, what these individuals conceive of is available to them singly, in each individual case, only through the prior operation of external social causes that shape the mind and provide its contents. Remember that we are speaking here only of the first threshold of action; we are far from having in mind the several crossings on the way to a completed act. At this point, therefore, any formulation of the "psychic imagination" may seem to ignore the hard, fast, and sometimes rigid social environment that Freud called the "reality-principle."

As action proceeds to cross the later thresholds, there is ample opportunity for the "reality-principle" to assert itself. At the second threshold the individual encounters the resistance of others' orientations; remember, for example, the illustration of the story, the "road to Emmaus," in which the disciples' orientation to the crucifixion (i.e. as a tragedy or failure) came into conflict with the purpose of that event from the narrator's point of view: a viewpoint presumably close to that of the one who was crucified. The purpose of any action, arising from the actor's original will, inevitably comes into harmony or conflict with the purposes of others who concern themselves with a particular action; in that relationship there is ample room for misinterpretation to distort the actor's original will or to defeat it. The third threshold places an actor in another situation of potential conflict with reality; there is no guarantee that the public will respond appropriately or supportively to an individual, regardless of how authentic or meaningful the action was to its immediate audience and recipients. To engage the public in taking such actions seriously is one function of ritual, where responses are prescribed, obligatory, and usually given in appropriate fashion; even a rite, however, is no guarantee that an action will take on significance to those who were not original witnesses. The development of religious reflection on the crucifixion suggests how far an action must travel to cross the threshold from the initial and immediate to the most public social context. However, even there (e.g. in the ritualized expression of responses to the crucifixion in the Eucharist) the act is not wholly finished; it is part of a world which cannot respond in kind and therefore awaits an eschatological conclusion. Until the fourth threshold is crossed, questions of reality still intrude; and until a community of faith or knowledge completes an act according to its own requirements for falsification, the truth question remains unanswered. In the case of the Christian community, those requirements await the end of history.

As an aid in understanding what I mean by "reality" at the first threshold, consider a prototypical individual: a fictitious primitive, perhaps, or a child whose view of the self and the world is not yet highly complex, articulated, and therefore open to correction and completion because it is fragmented and full of pieces that somehow do not fit the picture as a whole. (There is a debate on the amount of logical or scientific reasoning of which the hypothetical primitive was capable, just as there is a debate on how advanced are the reasoning capacities of a prototypical modern individual; I do not want to enter that debate in this context.) The mind of this putative primitive is a mixture of motives and intentions – not all of them conscious, by any means, but all of them comprising two whole sets. On the one hand is a set of motives that can be catalogued with the aid of psychoanalytic categories: magical thoughts, aggressive and incestuous wishes, panic, anxiety, fear, and a hunger for fusion with the environment or for connection and mastery; images of the self that derive partly from fears and partly from wishes, from memories but also from fantasies; the catalogue goes on. If that suggests one set within the mind (call it "motive"), the other set consists of intention. While "intention" is equally indebted to memory and fantasy, outlived wishes and unrealistic ambitions, it also includes orientations toward the world that I have already discussed under Parsonian headings – a set of orientations toward objects in the world as gratifying or as useful. These orientations may depict situations in relation to an individual's wishes or strategies for achieving certain goals. The same set of orientations may view the world as a source of standards or a basis for commitments. The primitive, in this hypothetical case, constructs a mental "world" from bits and pieces of these two sets (motive and intention). It is to this "world," I suggest, that Edelson refers when writing of "psychic reality": "reality as constructed by the activity of the mind; there is no other reality that man can know" (Edelson 1976: 159).

In choosing the hypothetical example of a "primitive", I intended to suggest that the construction of this psychic world into a single set from the pieces of two sets (motive and intention) is the achievement of will. Will, however, depends to some extent on how coherent or fragmented, how complex and highly articulated, the social world actually is. Intentions also will reflect to some degree the reality-testing capacity of the individual. If the modern world emphasizes skills, each located in a specialized and narrowly defined role, the intentions of the individual will no doubt reflect these roles as parts of a set of constraints and opportunities. If the modern world locates activities in large, complex organizations and governs them by rules that are largely explicit, precise, and highly codified, the intentions of the individual will no doubt be aware of these standards (to the extent that the individual is oriented toward the world as a source of such standards). Finally, so long as the world offers values that are highly abstract, like competence, excellence, efficiency, or symbols that refer to distant or somewhat fictitious entities (e.g. the nation as a source of commitments), the individual will incorporate some of these symbols and values in the set of intentions. The modern world does indeed require more highly developed ego-functions than a less complex world, although it might well be that the primitive could not have survived without highly effective ego-functions (see Weinstein and Platt 1973: 39). The point is that, at this first threshold, the individual creates a world that is psychic and which mixes the distant or the familiar with the most intimate and personal in a more or less coherent whole.

It is this psychic reality of which religion is perhaps more critical than it is of sin itself. This is the world of *maya*, illusion; this psychic reality is what the New Testament refers to as *sarx*, "the flesh". Although *sarx* or "the flesh" has modern connotations of the carnal or material, to the early Church "the flesh" included ambitions and wishes, intentions and motives; these might be oriented toward social status, recognition, or power rather than to purely material things. The offense, to the religious conscience, is that one achieves a closed set of motives and intentions that constitutes itself as the world; it is a world of its own or unto itself – closed, and therefore an offense against the truth regardless of how real it may seem or of how many others may reinforce the individual's psychic reality. That is why I prefer the position of sociological realism that distinguishes "truth" from a "reality" that is both social and psychic but *only* that. Take, as an example of a psychic reality oriented toward "higher things," asceticism itself. As Weinstein and Platt note, asceticism renounces the satisfaction of certain instinctual drives (Weinstein and Platt 1973: 41–2). It is indisposed toward "maintaining the actual presence of complementary ideal objects" (p. 42). Asceticism itself, however, creates precisely that set of motives and intentions derived from the two sets I have mentioned: a set that becomes a coherent orientation toward reality. The New Testament gives such "spiritual exercises" little credit for making the individual whole, and in any event the early Churches consistently renounced efforts by the individual to achieve, precisely as an act of the individual, such a private form of righteousness, a righteousness of one's own. On the contrary, the religious aspiration toward a completed act warns precisely against the premature foreclosure of the consciousness at this initial threshold of action.

Impediments to Crossing the First Threshold: Temptation

There is one more barrier impeding action before motive and intention can be integrated. The first is sin: a mixture of anxiety and unbelief that underlies the best of intentions; and the second is the psychic reality that I have referred to here in biblical terms as the "flesh" or *sarx*. The latter is the world: a psychic reality that achieves premature unity and simplification of both the self and the environment. The third is what might be called temptation itself: the temptation to return to motives that have not been fully renounced and threaten in any case to give the lie to one's best intentions.

An example from a religious rite may help to summarize the relation of these three impediments to each other. At the first threshold the individual signifies the synthesis of motive with intention by a sign; a sign is the primary means of communication at this threshold of action, and it stands for the will. An example of such a sign is easily found in the rite of baptism, an initiation that signifies the individual's will to engage in action that is complete and irreversible. A sign of that will is given in baptism; one recent wording speaks of the rite itself as "the outward sign by which we receive for ourselves what he has done for us" (*Alternative Service Book*, p. 229). In other words, the rite of baptism allows individuals to orient their lives within the framework provided by one final, complete act (the one proclaimed in the New Testament). Here I also mean by sign something more immediate and literal; for example, the sign of the cross made on the forehead of the initiate by the priest at baptism. In taking on that sign, the individuals that are being initiated are told to renounce sin, the first impediment; they are also told to renounce the world (and also used to be required to dispense with the flesh), the second impediment. In the baptismal rite the third impediment is referred to as evil or the devil; it is the temptation to act on motives that one has disavowed but that may overwhelm even very good intentions. These three are "the powers of darkness" from which the initiands are to be delivered by the prayers of the faithful. The third is perhaps the most serious impediment because it comes to the individual as though from the outside in the form of temptations, though the power of that temptation is the inward motive that has not fully been renounced.

Take, for example, the power of the aggressive motive. It may be renounced by an intention to be obedient. The same intention may make that same motive sublime. Instead of wishing to have a strong impact on the world, to be a "hit," the individual may intend to make a good impression instead of an impact, and instead of being a "hit," so to speak, the individual may adopt the more sublime intention of taking part. Participation and involvement can disguise and yet give indirect or symbolic satisfaction to the desire to make a dent in the world. One owes the world either a kick, so to speak, or a more acceptable expression of the social obligation to give the world its "kicks." Aggressive motives may be diverted onto safe objects; one can do battle with Satan and the forces of (outer) darkness. Finally, as a defense against these internal forces, one can claim to be helpless and dependent on powerful, loving figures for protection; no possible threat can arise from a supplicant figure. All of these strategies for disguising, minimizing, sublimating, redirecting, and stepping backward over the motive of aggression can be found in the rite of baptism. There the individual falls back on the protection of the Church and of God, in whose life the individual seeks to participate. The individual promises to be an obedient soldier as well as a servant – a soldier whose fire is directed outward at the forces of evil rather than at the authorities of the Church itself. There is a conflict expressed in this rite, and it is indeed a war; hence the initiands are enjoined to "fight valiantly." The war is one in which the individual is directed to be wounded, to suffer, and to die in the struggle with evil; indeed, the rite itself speaks of being "made one with Christ in his death" as a means of taking action across the first threshold toward final consummation (see *Alternative Service Book,* p. 231). The danger, of course, is that the aggressive motives foresworn in this rite or directed outward toward evil elsewhere, will reassert themselves in intentions of which the Church and the state would not approve.

Of course, modern societies are too complex to offer a single target for motives of aggression. The more complex nation-states are tied together more by rules or temporary political exchanges than by any enduring emotional ties or broad agreement on values. In the

normal course of social life, individuals therefore find their relationships cool, specialized around specific tasks, temporary, and impersonal even where the rules of the relationship call for the individual
to reveal personal information. Such a society is not likely to foster
any delusions of collective grandeur; neither is social life of this sort
likely to sustain illusions of safety or belonging. Under these conditions even intimacy is increasingly pursued according to rules
learned informally in the competitive struggle for friendship and love
or, more formally, under the guidance of popular experts in winning
friends, influencing people, or managing responsible exchanges.
Magical aspects of thinking find little expression in social life beyond
the individual's own routines − practices that may become increasingly obsessive as individuals try to compensate for increasing feelings of isolation and helplessness. If the typical mental illness in such
a society is not obsession, it may well be a widespread and chronic
narcissism that makes individuals profoundly uneasy when in the
company of intimates, for fear they will be hurt, and profoundly
anxious when alone, for fear they will be abandoned (see Lasch
1980). It is not a comfortable society in which to be vulnerable or
old. Whatever insecurities remain from childhood in any adult will
be stimulated again and again by the competition, fragmentation,
and uncertainty of social life in a society that resembles an arena
rather than a family. The underlying anxieties of childhood are thus
reinforced by the anxious concerns of adulthood; underneath whatever serenity or reasonableness the adult can intend lie the more or
less unresolved anxieties of childhood; these early motives precede
and undermine the acquisition of faith.

Of course, no ritual can prevent aggressive motives from coming
into play even when individuals appear − to all intents and purposes
− to be rational. The baptismal rite I have just mentioned seeks to
sublimate aggression or direct it toward appropriate targets. The
more ritual fails to deflect or sublimate aggressive motives, the
more likely are the best intentions to have a regressive character.
Individuals who suffer may well yield to the temptation of making
others suffer with them through the routines of professional practice, office management, the processing of clients, and the making or
administration of public policy. Amiable political leadership deflects
criticism from public policies that are in effect sadistic in broadening
the distribution of misery among more politically vulnerable social
strata. Under these conditions, the consequences of individual

actions are both more widespread, indirect, impersonal, and more difficult to identify precisely because they occur in the routine course of social life.

Ritual enjoins individuals not only to sublimate their aggression and to care for others but, in the case of the rite I have just mentioned, to depend entirely on divine love and protection or on the care of the family of God. A complex and impersonal society, however, makes such a sacrifice of aggressive impulse even more risky. Precisely as the nuclear family gives way to smaller units less able to sustain their members, the more individuals seek politically to turn the larger society into a surrogate or pseudo-family. The intense reactions to the keynote address at the 1984 Democratic National Convention in the United States signify the public demand for a social system in which one person's struggle stimulates public effort, as a family struggles together to support the efforts of its individual members. As the "magical" aspects of social life are pushed to the periphery by the routine and technical conduct of work and education, public pressure therefore mounts to restore prayer in the public schools and to educate children in "values." Society as a whole seeks to restore the very elements of mutual care and responsibility that have been lost in social life; this is the opposite of the process, more typical of the 1950s and 1960s, in which the system limits and corrects the intensely cohesive groups that provide havens for the individual. Without adequate rituals, however, metaphors will neither express nor evoke *commitment*. Without commitment, neither the Church nor any traditional community can effectively fulfill or challenge what is partial and distorted in the nation's life.

When rituals fail to synthesize aggressive motives with benign intentions, individuals may become increasingly dependent on their own devices for crossing this first threshold. Collective magic gives way to individual obsession which may take the form of compulsive concern with exercise, diet, personal growth and self-development, consumption and heightened states of consciousness in a society that offers no collective form of magical self-renewal. Under these conditions, ritualistic interaction may become even more important as a source of social, if not collective, reassurance; spontaneity will be administered in more limited or transient social contexts such as ideological or therapeutic groups, between audiences and celebrities, or in modernized religious rites. Under these conditions, sin precedes rather than follows guilt.

But Niebuhr points out that:

"By asserting these contingent and arbitrary factors of an immediate situation the self loses its true self. It increases its insecurity because it gives its immediate necessities a consideration which they do not deserve and which they cannot have without disturbing the harmony of creation."

(Niebuhr 1953: I, 252)

The true self cannot enjoy the wished-for significance and security by such attentive and repeated focus on the immediate social world.

The unsolved problem of uniting unacceptable motive with practical or legitimate intention leads the individual to construct a "world"; on this aspect of self-delusion, Niebuhr notes:

"If others will only accept what the self cannot quite accept, the self as deceiver is given an ally against the self as deceived. All efforts to impress our fellow men, our vanity, are revelations of the fact that it increases the insecurity of the self by veiling its weakness with veils which may be torn aside. The self is afraid of being discovered in its nakedness behind these veils and of being recognized as the author of the veiling deceptions."

(Niebuhr 1953: I, 207)

The implicit reference here is clearly to the fig-leaves and lies of the Garden of Eden that were of little use to defend the nakedness of the selves that had colluded to protect one another from their insufficiency, vulnerability, and manifest (when naked) incompleteness and separation. This self-delusion is what I earlier called the impediment of "the flesh"; it has its roots within the psyche at the moment of despair.

Rituals provide a way of taking the irrationality of individuals into account by conforming it to collective principles of order. When rituals fail to require individuals to own the impulses of hatred and murder in their own hearts, however, the hatred mobilized by social systems will remain inarticulate but effective. If Watergate took on the force of a national symbol, it was because Presidential animosities and vindictiveness remained concealed behind a stone wall of political rhetoric. The President had a list of "enemies," but his explanation of his actions emphasized their rationality. His office, he patiently explained, had to remain above partisan politics if it were to provide continuous and systematic guidance to domestic and foreign policy.

Behind this fine attention to procedural detail and the goals of rationality in public office was a man who made lists of enemies and went out of his way to injure them. There was little in his public rhetoric to indicate Nixon's vindictiveness, but the tapes from the Oval office told quite a different story. It is this same disjunction between high principle and covert operation that now dismays those who had put their faith in the current American President and believed that statements of principle would be adhered to in practice. At stake here is not only the tendency of human nature to disguise its weakness. It is the contrast between the public appearance of government claiming to be rational, principled and systematic, and its private reality.

Social life mobilizes passions that may be aggressive as well as affectionate, destructive as well as serviceable to life. Societies and institutions may therefore express murderous impulses without attending to them or without taking responsibility for them. One can act "as if" one is merely doing one's job or official duty when one is in fact acting out one's own hostile or aggressive wishes. By the making of policy one can act impersonally to create or destroy; one can make new categories of persons eligible for service or liable for punishment or ineligible for official consideration. King David once was censured by the prophets for his presumptions in enumerating the people in his domain, in an early taking of the census. In the United States, who will now judge the state for eliminating from its rolls thousands of individuals who, discouraged in the pursuit of jobs, drop from official enumerations of the "labor force" or, invisible in the inner city, drop from the census of citizens?

It is no wonder that critics have enjoyed a field day in comparing the continuous administration of modern bureaucracies with rituals. For instance, while bureaucrats hold office, clergy hold services according to the Office for Morning or Evening Prayer in the Episcopal Church. Both types of office must be performed without particular concern for the official's or clergyman's state of mind. Both require that the official in question go literally "by the book" and ignore, so far as possible, the sexual, ethnic, economic, and political characteristics of the people served by the particular bureaucrat or ecclesiastical office. Administration of the sacraments, like administration of the Internal Revenue Service, is regular, continuous, and *insofar as possible*, irrelevant to the personal ambitions and hatreds of the administrators. In the administration of large societies, however, there is far more opportunity for hostile motives to shape rational intentions than there is in any ecclesiastical rite which prescribes virtually every word and deed.

Rituals may allow grief and rage, hostility and greed to cross the threshold of consciousness where these emotions can find symbolic expression and relief. These passions are no less present for being subliminal in modern societies. In a subliminal state, however, they may be acted out in ways as harmless although incomplete as entertainment and sport, or indirectly in the more harmful but ritualistic routines of the office or marketplace, or through more direct forms of acting out in illness and violence. If the primitive survives in modern societies without the benefit and limits of adequate ritual, these destructive motives will cause untold damage and generate equally destructive motives of revenge.

More "primitive" societies enact in symbolic form irrational impulses of self-hatred, envy, rebellion, and murder (see Turner, 1969). The "enemy" or "victim" to be overcome or sacrificed may be anyone who threatens the individual's essential supplies of food, protection, self-esteem, and love. Modern societies, however, provide only a muted expression of murderous impulses in the smooth and ritualistic exchanges of a bureaucratized social life. Magical thinking and the impulse to eliminate all competition from one's life do not disappear, however, even when the modern adult learns to speak rationally about taking responsibility for one's own life. They may be haunted by persons they have left behind and by a self that they will never become; witness only the public fascination with journeys to outer space, with fantasy literature, and with video games that feature a haunted, pursued creature in a labyrinth. That labyrinth, whether it is the modern maze or the original creation of Daedalus, is still a fitting symbol of the unconscious and its tortuous control of our lives. In the absence of ritual, however, individuals must find their own personal pathway and absolve themselves of their own guilt. The lack of corporate absolution and of a common pathway leaves the individual with an unprecedented burden of responsibility without the promise of fulfillment or release.

The danger, then, is that personal grief and rage will accumulate without finding transformative channels in ritual for their public expression. As resentment accumulates, of course, it becomes more potent and liable to sudden explosion in ways that ignore whatever corporate forms of expression might yet be available. One therefore wonders not why there is so much violence, for instance, between blacks and whites but why there has been so relatively little. The danger increases that black rage, or white resentment, will take the form of direct and violent action rather than the dramatic but non-violent confrontations associated with the civil rights movement in the 1960s. It seems largely a question of time before the political vacuum is again filled with angry and destructive encounters. In the last weeks of 1986, as the proofs of this book were being read, New York City was the scene of racial beatings – one of them fatal – the first of which was initiated by young whites.

Conclusion

Even in a modern and complex society, to become an adult is to take one's parents' place and in some way therefore to imitate them. On the level of unconscious magical thinking, to take the place of one's father is to replace him and even to eliminate him. The unconscious can be terribly literal; this is why rituals are necessary to supply metaphors. One can then be serious and yet playful in acting out the unconscious themes of murder and sacrifice. In a ritualized society rites allow the community to recognize and deny the unconscious meanings of maturity; namely, that the person threatens to rival his or her ancestors. To overcome such an internal contradiction within the unconscious requires an extraordinary feat of acting *as if* one could both eliminate one's ancestors and keep them close at one and the same time. Rituals of initiation enlisted the aid of the unconscious in performing this feat by inducing various states of body and mind, as in the fatigue and ecstasy of the ritual dance itself. It was therefore no small thing to ignore or to impede such a work as the ritual dance, for then the unconscious can come into play on its own.

The collapse of differences between generations may therefore lead not only to an identity of hope and memory but to intense rivalry. As Girard puts it:

> "We have, then, a self-perpetuating process, constantly increasing in simplicity and fervor. Whenever the disciple borrows from his model what he believes to be the 'true' object, he tries to possess that truth by desiring precisely what his model desires. ... Whenever he sees himself closest to the supreme goal he comes into violent conflict with a rival."

(Girard 1977: 148)

Illustrations of this general thesis multiply in the literature of myth. Oedipus, who models himself on his father, comes into conflict with him precisely at the point where their paths cross: at the point where Oedipus desires what his father also desires. The succession of generations, necessary to the continuity of the group and the community, requires an identity of desire as well as of belief. No wonder that rituals in traditional societies provided symbolic gestures of violent destruction and safe objects for the venting of profound rage. The youths who came of age underwent severe trials in the time of testing. Even elders who succeeded to the throne found themselves scorned and attacked in gesture and rhetoric by their rivals and by their future subordinates but seldom, of course, destroyed in the process of accession to the throne.

The violence repressed and transfigured in these rites appeared also in funeral rituals. The elders who in death allowed their former rivals and subordinates to take the seats of power and authority in the family and the community found their ashes scattered in violent gestures, but their memories were held sacred. Rituals guaranteed the nonviolent succession of generations against the aggression stimulated by a common desire for the same objects and for symbols of power and authority. It is only in societies where religious authority fails to supply powerful metaphors for succession that it becomes expedient for one individual actually to die for the people.

In closing the social distance between generations, any society opens up the possibility of incestuous or patricidal acts. In ritualized societies the succession of generations was accomplished with what might appear to be unnecessarily expressive fanfare. The fanfare indeed suggests that sexual triumphs were being won, and violent emotions discharged, that might otherwise have destroyed the fabric of social life. More than one dynasty has been dissolved by the failure of ritual to provide appropriate satisfactions and substitutes for the ambitions and urges of a younger generation. To summarize, we turn back to Girard:

> "Rites of passage thus constitute a vitally important force in the conservation of institutions. They assure the dominance of generations long gone over generations yet to come. ... As always, it is a question of keeping the sacrificial crisis in check; in this instance, the concern is directed at the inexperienced neophyte whose youthful impetuosity could well unleash a new crisis."
>
> (Girard 1977: 285)

It may well be that the changes in modern societies make such powerful rituals no longer either necessary or possible. Modern rituals in which individuals come of age may fail to dramatize the transformation of the self, but the failure may not matter. Much less may be at stake, much less demanded of the initiate, and much less required in the way of transformation, since modern societies have multiplied the ways in which individuals can come of age. We now possess a bewildering combination of careers and stages by which individuals demonstrate competence and acquire authority. Because licensing, the acquiring of credentials, is a continuing process, it is difficult to know when one has arrived alongside a previous generation. The generations overlap and interpenetrate each other rather than imitate and replace each other. No wonder that individuals are confused about the nature of personal progress. There is no longer a single point at which the jealousy and competition engendered by individual growth make demands that only powerful rituals can meet. The process of maturing never ends, but neither does it usually culminate at critical moments for the society and the individual. Because individuals now have a wide variety of choices for making progress, they may pick and choose those with whom they will associate. Only those with a limited range of associates *and* with a limited set of choices for making progress are likely to need ritual as an alternative to acting out their aggressions or to getting sick with envy and anger. Why, then, does it matter that modern rituals are no longer adequate, especially when it appears that progress is no longer quite so problematical? There are two reasons for entering a cautious warning about the failure of ritual.

The first reason is simply that passions, once contained and expressed within rituals, are now allowed to remain unconscious *and* to be acted out in a wide range of areas of social life. Neither sports nor politics alone can keep those passions in reasonable bounds, since the inividual may seek to achieve victory or to suffer on a grand scale once acted out only symbolically in ritual. But whereas in traditional societies the victories over enemies in general and death in particular were won only in symbol, or at worst through limited sacrifice, in modern societies these victories may be sought on political or military fields of battle. The myths once contained within the limits of ritual now provide a language that may lend cosmic dimensions and meaning to otherwise secular conflicts. Under these conditions whole communities may be risked as conflict becomes sufficiently intense to threaten the destruction of all contenders.

Becker's description of the primitive, unconscious aspects of modern warfare is both appropriate and chilling:

"It seems that the Nazis really began to dedicate themselves to their large-scale sacrifices of life after 1941 when they were beginning to lose and suspected at some dim level of awareness that they might. They hastened the infamous 'final solution' of the Jews toward the closing days of their power, and executed their own political prisoners – like Dietrich Bonhoeffer – literally moments before the end. Retreating Germans in Russia and Italy were especially apt to kill with no apparent motive, just to leave a heap of bodies. It is obvious they were offering last-minute hostages to death, stubbornly affirming in a blind, organismic way, 'I will not die, you will – see?' It seems that they wanted some kind of victory over evil, and when it couldn't be the Russians, then it would be the Jews and even other Germans; any substitute scapegoat would have to do. In the recent Bengali revolt the Western Pakistanis often killed anyone they saw, and when they didn't see anyone they would throw grenades into houses; they piled up a toll of over 3 million despised Bengalis. It is obvious that man kills to *cleanse* the earth of tainted ones, and that is what victory means and how it commemorates his life and power: man is bloodthirsty to ward off the flow of his own blood. And it seems further, out of the war experiences of recent times, when man sees that he is trapped and excluded from longer earthly duration, he says, 'If I can't have it, then neither can you.'"

(Becker 1975: 111)

It is premature to assume that unconscious drives will always fall into place behind social arrangements. To be sure, the world has separated the place of work from the home where strong affections and rivalries intensify relationships. Accordingly, we might assume that sons and daughters no longer see the parent as so powerful an authority, since what remains of their economic and political power is now exercised outside the home. The same diminution of authority, it is assumed, accompanies motherhood in modern societies, where women are increasingly employed and the lore of parenting is printed in paperbacks available in the drugstore. These developments, I suggest, simply allow competitive and aggressive impulses to be sublimated, transferred, and displaced to a wider range of social situations. Mitscherlich puts it very well:

"The conservatism inherent in societies, which they do not lose even under the impact of revolutions, is rooted in the stubborn persistence of the earliest identifications, that is to say, the survival of the magical pattern of experience associated with the earliest stages of life side by side with later patterns of experience in which there is a larger element of conscious critical control. Societies consist of individuals all of whom have passed through these phases of development, and a substantial amount of magical thought, anchored in the super-ego, survives as a regulative factor in the attitude to the world and to the self. In particular, the patriarchal structural components of our society are closely associated with magical thought. It assumes the omnipotence–impotence relationship between father and son, God and man, ruler and ruled, to be the natural principle of social organization. Historical development, however, has been marked by a strengthening of the conscious critical capacities, which have relativized the omnipotence–impotence relationship. This makes filial dependence and paternal authority no longer seem to be necessary and permanent, but concessions subject to revision."

(Mitscherlich 1970: 145–46)

The succession of the generations still requires that the older generation be replaced, and there is still murder in the unconscious. The aggressive or sadistic drives can now be acted out symbolically or with more direct effect in every office, agency, and institution. As values and loyalty become generalized, so does the capacity to inflict or endure suffering. If Elvis Presley is – or was – "king," as many of his followers have insisted, some other king has been dethroned; there is no doubt of that, if the logic of myth offers us a guide to the collective expression of unconscious wishes. Swanston makes the point very simply:

"No myth can, not even the myth of Osiris and Horus where the kingdoms are carefully distinguished, contain both a father who is an almighty Lord and a son who is King of his people. Theologians generally have seemed to suppose their opening articulation of an almighty creator to be unaffected by their later articulation of belief in a kingdom without end for his own son. But the elaboration of the Christological section has in fact come near to dethroning the Father at the triumph of his Son."

(Swanston 1976: 103)

In the next chapter I will point out once again that in a modern society competition and conflict can be compartmentalized to some extent, and individuals may consciously choose among many options for progress. Grant that modern societies have found ways to provide these opportunities for progress and innovation without *directly* threatening the authority of the previous generation. In part this accomplishment depends on separating one field of endeavor from another; hence the importance of entrepreneurial activities, or of research or development as separate aspects even of a modern corporation. No less important is the separation of family life, where parental authority may remain intact, from the occupational world where parents may find themselves in direct competition with their children. Grant also that the multiplication of possible careers and the separation of many kinds of work into different public or private organizations minimizes the threat, posed by all progress, to the continuation of cherished associations with friends and family. Still it remains true that motives for domination and needs for help linger in minds that otherwise appear wholly reasonable and progressive. On the level of the unconscious, as in myth, there is still only one enemy and one reward. That is why it is so important, both for the individual and the society, for motive and intention to be harmonized as far as possible in a single will.

If this warning about the failure of ritual is muted, it is because troubles in one area of modern society do not usually have an impact elsewhere. In more highly differentiated societies, passions are more easily contained wherever they are expressed within the limits of the family or a modern corporation, whereas in simpler societies those passions, being more diffuse, were more easily expressed in ritual. Now, whether one is happy or rewarded by associations at home or among playmates, one can still make progress at work, and problems at work may not threaten one's other associations. Compared with simpler societies, the modern world is in fact more highly differentiated and able to contain or disperse disruptive passions.

In more complex societies, moreover, the younger generation may not wish in every way to emulate its elders. The young can make progress at work without trying to possess the objects of common desire. Under these conditions rituals may have less "work" to do in sublimating and displacing drives that may otherwise lead to conflict or violence between the generations. Mitscherlich's thesis that modern societies provide bureaucratic channels for aggressive behavior attests to the radical separation between the aggressive desire to succeed and the desire to possess common objects (Mitscherlich 1970). In a society that provides multiple careers as channels for aggressive impulses, the desire to succeed may not cause quite the same intensity of competition as in a society which requires the displacement of one generation by the other. The raising of the retirement age, the proliferation of occupations, and the opening of careers outside these occupations provide multiple pathways to attainment and recognition. These differentiated activities provide the outlets for competitive desires, whereas ritual once contained the inevitable rivalry and aggression between generations.

Ritual is left with a somewhat easier task of guaranteeing a non-violent succession when a society sublimates and displaces violence onto a wide variety of symbolic or other objects. It is not surprising, therefore, to find in many modern rituals, introduced by Catholic and Protestant churches within the past two decades, a muted and even banal expression of guilt for dangerous thoughts and feelings. The old confession, with its anguished expression of guilt for unhealthy and dangerous impulses, seems overdone in a society with such a proliferation of safe roles as outlets for desire and as opportunities for success without succession.

Nonetheless, ritual, because it taps the unconscious, provides an opportunity for the unconscious to break through the ordinary states of consciousness suitable for plowing and planting, working or making decisions. Ritual does not necessarily lead to ecstatic or sublime levels of conscious experience. In any ritual event, however, old animosities and affections, long repressed, are able to break through into symbolic action or even, in some cases, into direct love-making and sacrifice. When the unconscious breaks through into direct action, however, rituals contain the eruptions within certain limits of propriety and of time and space; the damage is perhaps limited to one who dies for the satisfaction or preservation of the people. The point is simply that ritual is eventful partly because the unconscious, more or less sublimated, finds its way out of the labyrinthine and interconnected pathways constructed by a repressive consciousness to contain powers felt to be so potent, fertile and destructive. Rituals allow the bull of the unconscious to enter the china shop of institutions with minimal damage. The experience can be invigorating for the institutions and at least temporarily satisfying for the devotees.

There is a second reason to be wary of a society that fails, through ritual, to provide satisfactory expression of unconscious motive and (good) intention. Succession from one stage in life to the next does not always occur on schedule; for some the succession of life-stages is always too abrupt and difficult, and in the 1960s there was little that was effortless in the way an entire generation of young people came of age. When a generation ages too quickly, the transition is often violent, and even the normal course of activities seems meaningless or oppressive.

In the next chapter I will point out that when educational curricula cease to offer a course to follow and become a set of options, the succession of work and play becomes problematical. Too many choices and too few requirements make any action incomplete; one never knows when one has done enough or what one has accomplished. So long as individuals go quietly from work to play, job to job, and course to course, their underlying doubt and anger at facing a bewildering array of meaningless or hopeless choices need not surface. That hostility may never achieve social importance and may become merely a chronic, widespread disenchantment of the sort described by Lasch as "narcissism."

In some cases, however, the boundary between work and play disappears. For the experience of this extremity, Erikson (1959) has given us a phrase, "identity crisis." Individuals who experience a breakdown in their ability to move from one stage in life to the next turn night into day; the normal succession of activities fails to engage them. At any given moment they may not be sure what to do next, and they are notably unsure what to do with their lives. They seek an all-or-nothing fusion with roles but fail to find a role to which they can make a total commitment. Individuals in "identity crisis" want everything to make sense; nothing else will do, and they would prefer nothing to a life which only makes partial sense. Under these conditions and for these people, ordinary roles fail to enable them to take their place in the succession of generations, and even rituals fail to inspire faith and give conviction. In the next chapter I will discuss this as a problem in crossing the second threshold of action: a failure to find meaning in the relation of one's own purpose to those of others.

When some individuals find the ordering of activities and stages of life no longer meaningful, routine decisions take on existential, life-and-death significance. At such times, individuals may seek to resolve their crisis at the second threshold by returning to the first and seeking personal transformation. Individuals in such extremities may choose to enter any one of several highly ritualized social contexts, from the army to a religious sect. To spend a few years of one's life in a highly ritualized society, whether sacred or secular, may be essential for certain individuals in crisis; otherwise the individual is immobile and paralyzed. Military organizations and sectarian groups may serve well to help a society to raise mature individuals and to enable one generation and regime to succeed another.

4

Crossing the Second Threshold: From Many Voices, One Meaning

Earlier I mentioned the discussion that took place, according to New Testament sources, on the road to Emmaus: a discussion of the meaning of the crucifixion. In that discussion the purpose of the one who was crucified seemed to have conflicted with the purposes of his followers; the meaning of that action was therefore at stake. For an action that may be self-sacrificial to be construed as an act of self-sacrifice requires more than a knowledge of the individual's intentions and motives; even if they are fully known and understood, an actor's will alone does not give an action meaning. An action whose purpose is self-sacrificial may be understood by disappointed friends and followers as a suicidal act; to the individual's detractors and enemies the same action may have seemed vengeful or foolhardy at best. In the case of any action, therefore, more than one purpose is involved; there are also the purposes of other actors who were intended to be the beneficiaries or victims of an action: its intended audience, recipients, and eventual respondents. Here I am primarily concerned with the purposes of the audience and recipients. On the relation of their purposes to the purpose of an individual actor depends the meaning of an act in its own place and time.

Meaning is therefore always problematical because no single purpose is definitive. In the case of the crucifixion, not even the purpose of the crucified one was sufficient for determining the meaning of the act; certainly the purposes of his followers and friends were not definitive. What occurs in that conversation is a combination of several voices: the voice of the crucified, the voices of his friends and followers, to be sure, but also the voices of the prophets as these are reported indirectly by the stranger along the road. The voices of the prophets, furthermore, reported their own conversations with God; and there are traces in the conversation at Emmaus of the voice of the divine – traces, of course, that are only indirect even as initially recorded, rather than direct and spontaneous like the voice of the companion whom the disciples have met along the way as he reminds them of the prophets' expectations and message. In the traces and relations of all these voices, then, the meaning of the crucifixion begins to emerge. No single voice is definitive or effective apart from its relation to the others, and the others may themselves incorporate words that were spoken in other times and places. In this layering of speech emerges the relation of one purpose to another until a meaning emerges that can be adequately symbolized. At Emmaus, of course, the symbol was the act of breaking bread and eating that initially had also summarized and conveyed the meaning of the crucifixion at the Last Supper. If the crossing of the first threshold of action requires the use of a sign, it is a symbol that marks the crossing of the second threshold separating an action from a complete and irreversible act.

The more problematical the relationship among these purposes, the more likely are the other voices to be heard before the relationship becomes meaningful. Consider how many voices were heard from in that narrative: not only the participants in the immediate conversation, but through these participants the voices of prophets and of the divine. The more problematical the purposes of those present, the more likely it is that the actors involved will draw on the speech of others who are not directly party to the conversation. As I will show toward the end of this chapter, the Liturgical Commission of the Church of England turned to a variety of expert and external voices to resolve differences represented in the purposes of its own members.

To put it another way, the more that direct speech is unable to resolve the differences among several purposes, the more likely it is that conversation will fall back upon indirect speech to derive meaning from differing purposes. That is, after all, what goes on normally in everyday life and in more formal contexts such as a trial, where differences among purposes are expressed and perhaps resolved through recourse to others' testimony.

Differences among purposes become problematical when there is apparently no single point at which a common purpose can be articulated. Where purposes fail to converge, individuals use indirect speech to find a symbol that incorporates multiple, although potentially compatible, purposes in reports that are implicit commands. Where the purposes are clearly in conflict, the use of indirect speech will report voices that are more explicitly commands. While I will not be able to prove any of these propositions from a single case, the example of the new Anglican rites will provide some interesting illustrations. The multiple and often conflicting purposes represented in the Liturgical Commission were articulated in voices that were both direct and indirect and incorporated commands that were both explicit and implicit. The final texts represented a meaning that was sufficiently complete and coherent to be translated into other times and places; that is, to be published. The problems of transferring meaning from one context to another will concern us in the next chapter as we take up the third threshold of action; here we are looking at the ways individual actors aggregate and resolve their many and often conflicting purposes into a meaning that can reside in an image or a text that will convey that meaning to beneficiaries of the action not initially present.

Of course, there is no guarantee that an action will successfully cross the second threshold and acquire a meaning that incorporates, validates, reconciles, and transcends the several purposes of the individuals most directly involved in the action itself – no guarantee even in ritual itself. For meaning to emerge from multiple, ambiguous, partially related, and potentially conflicting purposes a symbol is required that meets these criteria. The symbol serves no single actor's purpose at the expense of others' purposes; all purposes are included in that symbol. The same symbol will serve no unknown or ulterior purpose; all relevant purposes have been disclosed. That symbol will be understood as "true" and not only "real." The symbol not only enshrines a meaning, in other words, that is socially constructed (and therefore real in the Durkheimian sense that we have discussed in the Introduction); it may also be true in that same Durkeimian sense in which all social facts, no matter how dependent they are initially on social conditions, may be "true." There is no relevant purpose not included in that symbol; neither does the symbol have a meaning that cannot be translated into a relevant purpose. That is what I have in mind when I argue that action, in crossing the second threshold, takes on meaning.

Certainly an action will find it more difficult to cross the second threshold toward meaning if the actor's will is not clear (first threshold). An action may be later undertaken according to a purpose in which the underlying motive conflicts with the stated intention: a flawed will. I have discussed that possibility in the previous chapter under the heading of sin. Wherever unbelief, anxiety, or outright deception undercut an action, its purpose will not easily or completely be related to others' purposes. Individuals will engage in what Berger (1963) has called "bad faith"; intentions that fit within accepted social frameworks are based on or disguise motives that are contrary to the intention. To act purposefully may therefore disguise a motive to avoid responsibility, and an action that is intentionally self-sacrificial may in fact be based on motives of hatred toward the self or others. Without rehearsing the argument of the previous chapter, it may be enough simply to mention two other problems that may be residually active at the second threshold, although they derive from the first: an inability to transcend one's own world enough to entertain the purposes of others, and a desire to act out motives or intentions that one has apparently outlived or repudiated. The flesh and temptation – like sin – may inhibit the crossing of the second threshold if the framing of purpose has not already made them inoperative.

An action has completed the crossing of the second threshold when the relation of the several purposes of the actors becomes clear – clear, at least, to all relevant actors, audiences, and recipients, although later beneficiaries and respondents have yet to come into the picture. At Emmaus, the symbol of the meal establishes in the minds of the disciples the relation of their purposes to the purposes of the one who was crucified; that relation had become clear in the interplay of their voices with those recorded and reported earlier as the voices of the prophets, an interplay made possible and sponsored by the voice of the strange interlocutor who had joined them along the way. The crossing of the second threshold involves the revelation of meaning from the juxtaposition and interplay of a variety of voices whose relation only becomes sufficiently clear in the giving and receiving of a symbol; in the Emmaus case, the symbol of the meal confirmed the warming of their hearts as the stranger had been speaking to them. That meal was the beginning of a new rite; it is fitting, then, that in the latter part of the chapter we investigate the making of new liturgical texts to see what common meaning emerged there to relate many disparate purposes.

That symbolic meal (Emmaus) had some of the earmarks, so to speak, of ritual. Certainly the New Testament provides a context in which the reader of this account will relate that meal to a variety of other symbolic meals: the feeding of the 5,000 in the wilderness, the Last Supper, the resurrection appearances in which Jesus eats fish or bread with the disciples, the sacramental meals of the early Christian community, and finally the sacrament of the Eucharist itself. The correspondence of this action with ritual will concern us in more detail shortly; certainly I would not want to argue at this point that no action can cross the second threshold without ritual or that all rituals succeed in facilitating the crossing of that threshold. There are other passages besides those provided by rites, and some rites fail. Here the point is simpler: that a symbol or text can give meaning to the relation among purposes only when all relevant actors, audiences, and recipients of an action agree on the meaning of the symbol itself. These symbolic meals act as a paradigm for the relation among divine and human purposes. The paradigmatic symbol makes it possible for the actors, audiences, and recipients to agree on the relation of their several purposes; in this case, they all exhibit and are subordinate to the divine purpose in the Incarnation.

On Texts and Societies: a Theoretical Statement of the Question, "How can a single, homogeneous text emerge from a complex society?"

To put it another way, consider the crossing of the second threshold as the place where theory is born. As two sociolinguists have recently argued, one can view "theory as the revelation of many speeches in the form of a discourse which bears the trace of many speeches" (Silverman and Torode 1980: 206). There are several advantages to viewing the emergence of meaning as the birth of theory. Certainly sociologists have looked on theory as the discerning of the relation among different aspects of social life, and all social life consists of purposeful action rather than random behaviour. After all, in ritual one can actually see individuals and their representatives acting out their various purposes in relation to one another. The authors also have in mind another advantage of viewing the emergence of meaning as the origin of theory: theory becomes an exercise of the critical intelligence in which individuals see not only what is but what might be the interplay of disparate and perhaps conflicting purposes (Silverman and Torode 1980: 206). The order of things is not merely revealed at this stage; it is also shaped by the discourse and play of one voice after another. In this way a symbol emerges that takes on meaning by pointing to a level of meaning at which purposes come together: a new order emerging from the old.

There is one other advantage to using the word "theory" at this point. Actors become theoreticians fully as much as those who observe them. Of course, the boundary-line between sociologist, for instance, and actor is important for the maintenance of professional identity and self-respect; I am not proposing to dispense with it entirely. Nonetheless, I do wish to take my stand with those who see sociology as a practical activity because they also see individuals as being engaged in reflective, theoretical and critical activity while engaged in activities that are no doubt also practical and strategic, instrumental and adaptive. I have already explained (in the Introduction) why I side with Durkheim, say, in his criticism of pragmatism. Here I am drawing out one of the implications of the sociological position that society not only shapes and creates the individual but that the individual engages in the construction of social reality. Were that not true, it would be difficult for action to cross the second threshold, where meaning is not only given and received but shaped and created in the discourse and activity of everyday life.

Here I am speaking of what Halliday calls "the dynamic, inde-terminate nature of meaning" (Halliday 1978: 139). Following Halliday at this point, I would state as assumptions several points; they are axioms that give rise to the questions that I will pursue later in this chapter. Let us assume that "the exchange of meanings is an interactive process" (p. 140). Again, falling back on the example of a symbolic meal, I would argue that the exchange of meanings is precisely what occurred at Emmaus. Halliday speaks of such an exchange as a primitive potlatch in which gifts are given and received: gifts of meaning (I would add) that symbolize the relation of the actors' purposes to one another (p. 140). The gifts are given and received in everyday life and in formal ceremonies, in spontaneous speech and in written texts. In any event, the results are "acts of meaning" (pp. 140–41) that combine practical and pragmatic activities with actions that depend on and derive from a social system that they exemplify. The relation between societal and individual purposes is therefore interactive, dynamic, and creative. It is also, I would therefore suggest, fragile, contingent, and sometimes destructive: fragile, because the purposes of individuals and systems may vary greatly; contingent, because the effect of particular occasions and circumstances is often great; and potentially destructive because individuals can seldom muster together the power that a social system has more readily at its disposal. All of these variations and potential conflicts may inhibit the emergence of acts that have meaning.

The discussion can now begin to suggest how rituals may enable action to cross the second threshold. Let us return to the multiplicity of purposes, the sheer number of purposes that actors may bring to bear on each other. The number of these purposes reflects the degree to which a society is pluralistic in its goals and its values. Individuals may subscribe, for instance, to the stated educational goals of a school and so share the same purposes with regard to the curriculum, while at the same time they may have very different values and varying amounts of respect for the institution of education or the practices of a particular school (Bernstein 1975, Chs 1 and 2). In the same vein, I might add, schools may hold all of their pupils in the same regard so far as instruction is concerned but have varying amounts of respect for them according to a particular student's social class or ethnic background. Pluralism in such a society, I would suggest, leads to a higher number of options in the educational curriculum than might be found in a less heterogeneous society; the various experiments in "black" or "women's" studies and the increasing number of electives in the curriculum of American schools and colleges during the past two decades offer one case in point. How, then, does a pluralistic society seek to validate the disparate purposes of its citizens while yet bringing them together in a common framework where they might be shaped by a single paradigm? What symbol could possibly be adequate to express and direct such multiple purposes? Even the Liturgical Commission of the Church of England considered the possibility of producing liturgical texts to fit the "public school" and less advanced educational backgrounds of the laity, as we shall see later in this chapter.

In American schools, the inclusion of prayer has been one such effort at ritual; the pledge of allegiance has been another. Both efforts have become problematical, of course, and the use of both the pledge and of prayer has been contested in the courts. Judicial review is still proceeding, but it would appear that even a moment of silent meditation, obligatory for a class but optional for the individual student, has not passed inspection by the United States Supreme Court in 1985. On the contrary, even though the use of such meditation might be entirely symbolic and free from specific content, the use itself is problematical, given the constitutional sensitivity of education to controversies under the First Amendment. This is not the place to attempt to review the constitutional or political aspects of the issue; I am simply placing the use of such options in a social context where multiple meanings can be exchanged in ways that fail to cross the second threshold.

The introduction of new rites in a number of mainstream Protestant Churches offers a comparable example. If it were anywhere possible for a multiplicity of goals and values to be framed in a single rite, it would be possible, I suggest, in such large Churches that are relatively homogeneous in their clientèle and less susceptible to external review and challenge. Even in the new rites recently introduced in these Churches, however, the number of optional prayers in the text suggests that the term "common prayer" may be an anachronism. Certain standard prayers, for instance, have become optional where their use had been obligatory. More significant is the number of prayers that are included as options according to the needs and discretion of the actors who may be present at a given time and place. The prayers are like gifts that are exchanged between the members of a society in recognition of one another's purpose; as Halliday might also point out, the revision of the text accomplished by these Churches is continuous so long as different options are exercised from one occasion to another:

> "the Text is a continuous process. There is a constantly shifting relation between a text and its environment both paradigmatic and syntagmatic. ... And the ongoing text-creating process continually modifies the system that engenders it."
>
> (Halliday 1978: 139)

The process of creating a text is certainly continuous so long as options can be exercised, but whether or not the process "modifies the system that engenders it" depends on a number of other factors. In some societies it is obvious that the religious "left-hand," so to speak, does not know what the political and economic "right hand" is doing. In some of those societies, furthermore, it does not inhibit the effectiveness of the system as a whole that the two hands are not working together. Some societal purposes are not associated with others, and to some degree in any society the purposes of individuals are a matter of indifference to the system, and *vice versa*.

The Beginning of a Theoretical Answer to the Question on Text and Society: Two Propositions

The presence of multiple purposes in a society or smaller community is not intrinsically dangerous; multiplicity only breeds conflict when the purposes are irreconcilable and impinge on each other rather directly. In many institutions – notably educational ones – the purposes of those who teach and learn are no doubt divergent as well as different; those who fund such institutions and those who administer them also have mutually divergent interests. Taken together, these several purposes may be simply divergent and the actors bypass one another with occasional gestures of respect or hostility. Indeed, the paucity of ritual in such institutions suggests that the presence of many different purposes is not intrinsically dangerous to the survival of the collective enterprise. Of course, where strains are imported from the larger society, even educational institutions find themselves prone to disturbance, direct conflict, and occasional violence. Conflict between generations, ethnic groups, the sexes, and even between social classes may impinge directly on such institutions, and in the 1960s such conflict was pervasive in colleges and universities in the Western world. In times of scarcity, moreover, the purposes of academics and administrators may well come into conflict; the unionization of many faculties in American universities is a case in point. The issue is the extent to which multiple purposes are merely divergent, potentially in conflict, or directly opposed to one another.

The literature on social conflict is a sub-universe among sociological disciplines, and I claim no particular competence within it. Nonetheless, I will put forward here two propositions which concern the relation of divergent or conflicting purposes to the enactment of meaning. Take these propositions as statements to be developed to the point where they can be falsified "under certain conditions," and postpone for the moment, if you will, the question of what those conditions actually are. Here I am proposing a logical scheme that suggests some of the impediments separating purposeful actions from acts that have meaning.

The first proposition is simple enough. To the extent that multiple purposes are merely divergent, their expression in ritual will rely on a proportionate use of indirect speech. For instance, in the modern rites that I have been mentioning, it is clear that a number of "voices" are heard from directly in the form of a range of optional prayers. I would now simply add that a proportionate number of other voices may be heard from indirectly as other options are exercised in these rites; the new services of baptism, for instance, offer a menu of scriptural passages from which offerings may be selected according to the needs of the participants and the nature of the occasion. Assume, then, that the divergent purposes of the actors may find meaning to the extent that the voices reported indirectly in these scriptural passages serve the function that I earlier noted in connection with the Emmaus story; there it was the prophets' speech with its mixture of indirect and direct speech that provided a repertoire of voices from which meaning could emerge. The same function, I am suggesting, is provided by the repertoire of voices included in the alternative selections of Scripture permitted in the new rites. Of course, the older versions also provided selections and alternatives; the number and variety of choices have simply been enlarged to encompass the greater variety of purposes presumably coming into play in the constituents of the contemporary Church.

A brief selection of the rubrics governing the choice of readings in a modern baptismal service may suggest the level of complexity that has been reached in the rites; I have been suggesting that the exchange of meaning in these rites (e.g. through the choice and reading of various passages from Scripture) reflects and shapes the multiplicity of purposes in the society as a whole. Consider these rubrics from the baptismal service of the new English *Alternative Service Book*. The service opens with an option:

"1. At the entry of the ministers, this, or another APPROPRIATE SENTENCE, may be used: and a HYMN or a CANTICLE may be sung."

The service continues with a greeting (not optional) and another option:

"3. If the PRAYERS OF PENITENCE (Holy Communion Rite A, Sections 5–8) are to be used, they follow here.

5. Sit.
If an OLD TESTAMENT READING is to be read, one of the following may be chosen (see pp. 262–268).
[Eight O.T. passages are then listed].

7. If a NEW TESTAMENT READING is to be read, one of the following may be chosen (see pp. 268–271).
[Six N.T. passages are then listed]."

(pp. 227–28)

The service thus contains a prayer by the bishop (not optional), the command to sit (not optional), the Old Testament reading (optional), a concluding sentence for that reading (optional), silence (optional), a psalm (optional), a New Testament reading (optional), a concluding sentence for that reading (optional), more silence (optional), a canticle or hymn (optional), and an instruction to "stand" (not optional). All in all, of the fifteen actions that begin this rite of initiation, eleven are optional. The only requirements are the bishop's greeting (and people's response), the bishop's prayer, a command to sit, and a command to stand. These options allow for many voices to be heard from indirectly in psalm, canticle, and Scripture, reproduced in the context of the rite as though the voices were indeed living and present. The purposes represented in these options, however, are not only multiple but relatively undefined and divergent, with no suggestion of potential conflict. Like the curriculum of a modern college there are relatively few requirements and a multiplicity of electives. Those who administer and those who teach are apparently not at cross-purposes with one another, and those who are to be instructed or certified come with no contrary purpose to that of the institution, even though they may come with a number of purposes that are not easily expressed in terms of the curriculum or rite.

Now consider the second proposition: that when multiple purposes are potentially in conflict, not only will indirect speech be employed, but the element of command (whether direct or indirect) will be implicit. The voice of command is muted in these new rites, but it is there. The rite for the Eucharist notes, regarding whether one should sit or stand, that:

"when a certain posture is particularly appropriate, it is indicated in the margin. For the rest of the service local custom may be established and followed."

(*Alternative Service Book*, p. 115).

To establish local custom is a bit like training children to brush their teeth; the habit apparently does not come naturally and sometimes requires the threat of parental discipline if that custom is to be "established." A similarly unobtrusive level of command shows up in a rubric for the baptismal service. There it is pointed out that, even when children to be baptized "are old enough to respond," they will only answer the baptismal questions "at the discretion of the priest" (*Alternative Service Book*, p. 225). I speak of these exercises of authority as implicit commands, of course, because they rely on the apparent use of "custom" and of the priest's discretion. The order is nonetheless given or withheld according to the clergy's preference.

The implicit nature of the command structure is possible, I will argue, because of a structure in which purposes that are potentially in conflict and mutually interdependent are nonetheless compartmentalized. The purposes of the clergy and the parents of children are potentially in conflict: the parents wishing their children to be baptized and the clergy, perhaps, wishing the children to know what they are doing. There is other room for conflict, the clergy perhaps wishing whole families to be baptized together with the adults going on straight away to confirmation and communion, whereas the parents might wish for a separation of children from adults, a delay between one rite and another, or even for a private service rather than a public service which, in some parishes, is the Eucharist. There is a history here, in which the "Parish Eucharist" and the family have become the centers of parochial life in many congregations; I will not go into that history here, but it is widely available. The point is that the purposes of families and the single members of a congregation of one generation and another, and of those with varying preferences for the Eucharist as opposed to other offices may well come into conflict. That is why, I am suggesting, the new English rite for baptism and confirmation offers the following list of alternative occasions, each occasion requiring or permitting the use of a range of specific options for prayers, responses, and so on:

"• Baptism, Confirmation, and Holy Communion
• Baptism and Confirmation at Morning or Evening Prayer
• The Baptism of Children: at Holy Communion
         at Morning or Evening Prayer
• Confirmation with Holy Communion
• Confirmation without Holy Communion
• Confirmation at Morning or Evening Prayer"

These options for various occasions signify the presence of multiple purposes that are potentially in conflict. Because they are not mutually interdependent, however, they can be performed at various times and places and separated in the text by symbolic markers like letters or numbers. In this array of compartmentalized and specialized contexts, the rites reflect and help to shape the social structure of a complex society.

Later in this chapter I will go into more detail on the conditions which lead to such an organization of ritual and make it possible. It might help to refer briefly here, however, to the organization of work in a modern office building. There multiple activities go on in relative independence from one another. Many of these activities are highly interdependent in the long run; a failure in the accounting department may eventually arouse unwelcome interest by the Internal Revenue Service in the workings of top management. In the short run, however, these activities are far less interdependent than the work, say, of an assembly line that can easily be halted entirely by incompetence or mischief. In the office building, then, purposes are potentially in conflict but sufficiently autonomous to be compart-mentalized, and they are often compartmentalized in ways suggested by the organization of new rites: by markers that are movable, flexible, and highly suggestive of separate contexts and occasions. More on this subject later in the chapter; these are the conditions that make the second proposition realistic, and their absence would falsify that proposition.

Rituals and the Second Threshold

It is the work of ritual to make the competing purposes of many people have a meaning that can be evoked by a single symbol – a flag, perhaps, or a broken leaf. When rituals are being made, more-over, it is incumbent on the makers of a rite to frame their several purposes within a text whose meaning transcends and relates them all to one another with evident flaws and contradictions; if the makers of a rite fail, how can the rite succeed in binding many purposes into one? The work of the Liturgical Commission of the Church of England affords a particularly good example of how difficult such a task may be. On the one hand, being representative of some of the different constituencies of that Church, the Liturgical Commission reflected several purposes in its own composition: those of the modernizers and those of the promoters of the Church, those of the guardians of doctrine and the discipline, to mention

only a few. The more disparate its own purposes, moreover, the
more likely it is that the Liturgical Commission would seek to hear
from other, perhaps more indirect voices, in order to create a text
that would symbolize the relation of all these purposes to one
another; that, at least, is the burden of my first proposition. The
tendency of the Liturgical Commission to seek out other voices
comes out clearly in the following extract from the minutes of the
Liturgical Commission during their final meeting for the year 1966:

"LANGUAGE SUB-COMMITTEE REPORT
(Memorandum 72C)
The Chairman said he felt it might be unwise to put a 'patched'
revision such as the sub-committee had presented, before the
Convocations in an Appendix to the Report: it would only pro-
long debate. He had made contacts with various groups of experts
on music, journalism, linguistics and drama who would be pre-
pared to help the Commission by consultation and by considering
draft texts submitted to them and sending comment. He hoped
that texts such as that on Canticles (Memo. 74) might benefit
from further comment on the lines of the RADA notes (Memo.
74A) circulated at this meeting. He thought a booklet on the
various aspects of the language question might be helpful. Mr.
Ayerst asked if the Language Sub-Committee should cease, but
the Chairman hoped this Committee would continue its work."
(Minutes of the Liturgical Commission, Nov. 1966, Item 88)

In this brief excerpt from the minutes of the Liturgical Commission
we can see the Church turning to other voices to resolve its own
disparate (and perhaps conflicting) purposes. It is as if the Church
had concluded that outside authorities in various subjects could
instruct the Church on how to achieve various liturgical effects
through language. The Liturgical Commission and the Anglican
Church itself clearly lacked a social context within which certain
meanings and commitments could give force and authority to sacred
language. Indeed, the Church has come to the conclusion that there
is nothing so sacred about its language that experts cannot arrive at
independent and satisfactory conclusions concerning how the faithful should put their faith into words. The assumption implicit in the
move to call upon outside experts (in the above memo) is that the
Church's own resources are too limited – an assumption not entirely
lost on Mr Ayerst, who asked if the Sub-Committee on Language

should cease. Clearly the Liturgical Commission felt that to reach certain audiences (like those in the new housing estates) the Church should proceed to turn its language into a set of carefully contrived expressions to achieve the desired effect on outsiders who lack the Church's faith. Even the sacred can be rationalized, it would seem, into a series of means to particular ends, into an effective linguistic tool. That is not what I mean by a symbol (an image or a text) that can dramatize the relationship among disparate purposes and give them a common meaning.

The Church of England, in choosing to consult experts on the persuasive and compelling uses of language, clearly preferred the insight of expertise to the experience of the ordinary, faithful lay person. Lest there be any misunderstanding on this point, I will quote here another excerpt from the minutes of the Liturgical Commission, in which the Church's liturgists again choose to stay away from the grassiest of grass roots:

"(b) *Requests for Speakers* The Secretary requested that all members should supply her with as many names as possible of people who might be called upon to speak on liturgical matters. In view of the increased number of requests now coming to the office, and in view of the fact that members should not be troubled to speak to meetings smaller than e.g. a rural deanery, any suggestion of those willing and informed (e.g. members of diocesan liturgical committees) would be welcomed."

(Minutes of the Liturgical Commission, Dec. 1965, Item 37b)

It might help to understand the meaning of this decision if I pointed out that "deaneries" were the bodies which elected representatives to the Church General Synod. Like an electoral college, they stand between the individual voter and those who are elected to make the actual decisions that govern the Church's life. The Liturgical Commission was therefore a creation of a Synod that itself was elected to represent only the elected representatives (at the deanery level) of the ordinary church-member. Because the purposes to be framed in the new text were multiple and only vaguely articulated, the Church sought to resolve its differences by calling on a set of expert voices that had no clear relation to the voices that had called the Commission into being; not the voices of disciples, of the faithful, or of prophets, but of experts. The Liturgical Commission's decision to stay out of the local context was therefore a commitment to *abstraction* and *universalism* in thought and language that could only weaken the capacity of any new rite to tap the deep loyalties and commitments that emerge only when people have lived together over a long time and know each other in a variety of ways. While there were indeed members of the Liturgical Commission who from time to time put in a good word for honoring these loyalties and preserving the memories and language of the old *Book of Common Prayer*, their voices did not prevail.

In turning to other voices to relate their disparate purposes, the Church could consult several new translations of the Bible; these presented the Church with a number of options which have been passed on to the laity. It has therefore been difficult for any group of scholars and clergy to provide worshippers with a single text that would symbolize something "given" rather than manufactured, a unity among purposes rather than a reminder of their multiplicity. Precisely this problem confronted the Liturgical Commission of the Church of England early in their conversations over the language of what would eventually become the *Alternative Service Book*. The existence of alternatives for expressing the Christian faith always confronts liturgists with dilemmas of how to claim authority for their own version, but the dilemma has become more acute in recent years as the number of versions of the Bible has multiplied. With several biblical versions authorized for use in worship, no single reading or usage can claim unquestionable fitness or authority. Take, for example, the following entry from the minutes of the Liturgical Commission of the Church of England:

"LANGUAGE OF THE LITURGY (Memorandum 69)
... owing to Mrs. Montefiore's absence through illness only the following points were agreed: That 'you' should be used throughout for individuals apart from God, not 'thee'; and that the ending '-eth' should be avoided. But where either of these forms were used in a very familiar context (e.g. the salutation) they might be kept if *useful*. The Chairman said this matter could be raised again at the next meeting in connection with the language of Matins and Evensong."
(Minutes of the Liturgical Commission, Mar. 1966, Item 61; emphasis added)

Clearly the proliferation of biblical versions made it necessary to choose translations that rest on some authority other than the biblical canon itself. In this case the Commission made a decision to leave the choice open to the local Church, a choice that the Commission soon abandoned in favor of more expert or official opinion.

The choice of what is "useful" as a guide to choosing the proper forms of liturgical language makes sense for a type of authority that rests on a specialized division of labor, legalized controls, and individualized decision. That is a world in which individuals have a number of legitimate and reasonable options within each area of life, from working to raising children. It is also a world in which choices are made within specific contexts that do not necessarily impinge on other contexts. For instance, a choice to raise children may or may not be affected by where one works. As I noted in the second proposition, the compartmentalization of life in a differentiated society, along with the presence of options in each context, makes each decision apparently less interdependent with decisions made elsewhere, and the voice of "command" can be relatively implicit in the "report." New options can still be chosen, because what works in one context may not be obligatory or useful elsewhere. Organizational boundaries provide the limits and the context for individual choice, and individuals therefore need to worry less about trespassing over sharp and sacred symbolic boundaries.

The minutes of the same meeting of the Liturgical Commission provide another illustration of the Church's secular habit of mind, although on quite a different subject: the deconsecration of a parish church building. First, simply read through this excerpt from the minutes of that meeting:

"DECONSECRATION OF A CHURCH (Memorandum 68)
Introducing this Memorandum, Dr. Cuming said this matter was for lawyers rather than liturgists. Mr. Wigan said a service of farewell was what was needed, and the Provost of Derby added that it should include thanksgiving for the past uses of the church. It was *agreed* that the word 'deconsecration' should be avoided.

Other suggestions were made in further discussion. Convocations had never appointed a body to consider what deconsecration effected; lawyers required only the Bishop's signature on a document. The Commission should consider this matter in the future if requested. Normal usage should be to add the material on pp. 12–13 of the Appendix to the Memorandum to whatever service was to be the last in the church. A note on what scriptures would be appropriate should be added. Dr. Cuming agreed to present a shortened draft incorporating all suggestions to the next meeting."
(Minutes of the Liturgical Commission, Mar. 1966, Item 56)

Again, note the authoritative standards: legality, specialized knowledge, and utility. People who know about what is useful are more likely in this context to be lawyers rather than clergy; that is the clear meaning of Dr Cuming's remarks, even though other meanings, present in his speech, may not have survived in the text of these minutes. People who are parting with a place that is marked by familiarity rather than the sacred are quite right to say "Farewell" rather than to engage in an exorcism to drive out the spirits. "Thank you" and "Goodbye" will do. It is a familiarity that seems to breed a certain contempt for the authority of the sacred.

Take a moment to consider how different a service of this sort would have been in a simpler community, where the prayers of the faithful, the ashes and dust of the departed, and various spirits, would have made a particular place awesome in its power and meaning. The prayers and gestures of the living then would have been fateful not only for the passage of the departed but for the health and safety of the entire community. To deconsecrate such a place would have required something more than a friendly parting. The words and gestures would have been prescribed not by lawyers trained in what is useful for writing contracts, but by individuals who represented the entire community, its wholeness and salvation. In a complex world, however, one had better rely on lawyers than priests. Even the Liturgical Commission appears to take secularity for granted.

Here, then, is the situation in which the Church of England undertook to revise the language of worship; it is a situation shared by most denominations in the United States as well as in England. A specialized world has made the Church look on its own, sacred ways of speaking as one part of the division of labor in modern societies. If lawyers rather than priests need to be consulted with regard to deconsecration, the sacred no longer requires a special tongue; instead the requirements of utility and familiarity determine what is suitable. A complex society shrinks the scope of the sacred and of language that can convey the sacred. The Church's speech is now an institution's register or even the jargon of religious specialists. No wonder, then, that some thought the Church should worry about becoming more intelligible. The point is that no symbol was adequate to give meaning to the multiple and potentially conflicting purposes of liturgists, lawyers, and the laity.

In the following extract from the minutes of the Liturgical

Commission of September 1966 is a brief summary of some of their discussion of the "language" of worship:

"MODERN LANGUAGE IN THE SERVICES (Memorandum 69, 69A)

Mrs. Montefiore said it was impossible to divorce language from thought, and the mixture of modern terms with 'hath and doth' in e.g. the proposed draft Baptism was confusing. Though more care was needed on sentence-structure as well as word-forms, redrafting in new terms meant a change of attitude as well as technique, *with the consumer directly in mind.* The Chairman then spoke of comments from RADA staff on *bad rhetoric* in some modern-language versions. New drafts might be sent to RADA for comment on this point. Mr. Ayerst said the meaning of words must first be elucidated, so as to ensure intelligibility. *It was not true that even regular churchgoers necessarily understood the vocabulary with which they were familiar.* Perhaps 'Eleven-plus' type services (as well as 'public school'-type) were needed, in which only a controlled vocabulary would appear. *Many technical words have synonyms,* though some (e.g. 'grace') perhaps had not. Mr. Wilkinson said we must not close the door to poetry, but should help all to grasp the Bible and psalms as *basic tools of worship.* The Dean of Bristol said a small sub-committee should consider modern language and points such as rhythm-change in collects where 'You' replaced 'Thou' for God. Mr. Ross said that since the Revised Psalter had opted for 'Thou' the Commission should do likewise. It was agreed that a sub-committee consisting of Mr. Ayerst, Mrs. Montefiore, D. Brook and Miss Fraser should work on a short section of Memorandum 66 and report back.

When Mr. Ayerst reported back, he said there were three options open: to leave Memorandum 66 as it stood, to 'patch' *seriatim* by exchanging various words and phrases, and to redraft entirely. The sub-committee gave examples of some 'patches' but had left various phrases untouched pending advice from the Commission on the *precise theological ideas* that present words were intended to convey, e.g. 'inheritors of the kingdom of heaven', and 'sin, the world, and the devil.' He recommended that *modern alternatives should be presented* to the Convocations side by side with those in the Memorandum, thereby *giving them the option* to reject the modern forms *if they wished.*" (Minutes of the Liturgical Commission, Sept. 1966, Item 78; emphasis added)

There is no one saying, in this discussion at least, that the language of the Church belongs to the laity. On the contrary, according to Mr. Ayerst, many of the laity do not understand what they hear and say in Church and need instruction in a "technical" language. It is therefore unfortunate that the word "grace" does not have a synonym, although there is more chance of translating other important terms into language that the laity will comprehend. Behind this desire to change the terms of the laity's worship is an attitude that clearly reflects an industrial society in which producers seek a market for their products. Here Mr Wilkinson speaks of "the Bible and psalms as the basic tools of worship," and Mrs Montefiore speaks of the "consumer" in reference to the laity. The laity, then, is not in the business of producing its own worship, since liturgical manufacture has been consolidated in the hands of managers and specialists. While we need to be cautious in inferring too much of the thinking of the Liturgical Commission from such terminology, still it is true, as Mrs Montefiore points out, that one cannot "divorce language from thought."

The mechanical language of the Commission tends to oversimplify their task, since they themselves are faced with a bewildering array of options. The second paragraph of the excerpt quoted above speaks of "three options open" to the Commission, but each of these options leads the members to choose among the options presented by various Churches in their worship and by various translations of the Bible. It is not surprising that the Sub-Committee on Language wished for guidance from the Commission on "the precise theological ideas" that words such as "sin" or "kingdom of heaven" convey. It is revealing, however, that the sub-committee thought that such words were sufficiently technical in meaning to require and permit precise terminology. If such precision could be found in theological ideas, they perhaps hoped it would be simple enough to choose the correct linguistic tool for the task of conveying those ideas. In any event, "inheritors of the kingdom of heaven" is no longer a powerful metaphor for the people of God in history but a "precise" theological concept, a technical term. Further, the Church itself is no longer a powerful metaphor for the secular kingdoms of this world: a metaphor that corrects and completes what is implied in the notion of any (earthly) kingdom. Under these circumstances, where symbols are emptied of rich but imprecise connotation, it is impossible, I would argue, for a text to give meaning to the disparate purposes present in the Church.

The Decline of the Church as a Sacred Metaphor for Social Life

It is exceedingly difficult for the Church to be a sacred, authoritative metaphor for a society when its worship becomes a matter of choosing among many options. In simpler societies sacred words and places always involved profound loyalties and affections; it was critically important for action to cross the second threshold by giving meaning to purposes; in a less complex society, where each area of life impinges on all the others, meaning is crucial for the survival of the society. The need for meaning is therefore more individualized in modern societies where social life compartmentalizes religion, say, from work or the family. There individuals have a sometimes confusing array of options for personal or other growth.

In a complex social world, then, the Church offers small rather than large steps toward completing action into acts. Where the authority of the Church is secularized, the completion of actions is therefore more likely to be partial rather than total or what Erikson (1968: 74–90) calls "all or nothing." Because action consists of small steps forward without corresponding steps into the past to retrieve old portions of the self or to renew cherished associations with a prior generation, there seems little need for rituals that retrieve, renew, and transfigure the past in the present. Finally, where many options remain open even after a choice is made to pursue one line of action over another, rituals can hardly dramatize the imposed necessity of choosing the one and only right way into an opaque future.

Certainly the members of the Liturgical Commission were decided upon being reasonable and appreciative of the modern world; they did not want to place the believer in a situation that calls for dramatic, heroic, or radical choices between good and evil. The early discussions of the Commission on baptism, for instance, reveal the impact of a secular world on the Church's thinking about its own rites of initiation. The members of the Commission, during their meeting in December 1965 received "with interest" the text of a "draft liturgy" for baptism in the Episcopal Church of Scotland:

"They noted in general that the theological weighting of the material at the beginning seemed rather heavy, and felt that in England (e.g. in new housing estates) it might be hard to use."
(Minutes of the Liturgical Commission, Dec. 1965, Item 42a)

I have already noted that the Commission was thinking in terms suitable to an organization in a complex society and was therefore concerned with what might work or appeal to consumers in suburbs rather than in the more traditional areas of the country. Now it becomes obvious that this new social context seems inhospitable to the dark and heroic language of a baptismal rite that, in the traditional text, knows of original sin and everlasting damnation. At the same meeting the members of the Commission also suggested passages of Scripture suitable for a revised baptismal rite, and these passages are described in the following excerpt from the minutes. I have underlined a few words to suggest the half-hearted inclusion of scriptural references to "repentance"; such repentance has apparently become more of an option than a necessity for spiritual progress:

"(b) *Ministry of the Word* (cf. also *Memorandum 64*)

(1) After a long discussion it was agreed that 6 passages made this catena overlong. The Dean of Bristol presented an alternative version which was also discussed, and the whole was remitted for redrafting with the suggestion that at least the four following elements be retained: (a) a reference to our Lord's baptism in Jordan: (b) the text of our Lord's command (Matthew 28): (c) a reference to John 3, in which the words dealing with the kingdom would lead to (d) the text of Mark 10 on children. *If possible, Acts 2 with its reference to repentance was also recommended for inclusion.*"

(Minutes of the Liturgical Commission, Dec. 1965, Item 466; emphasis added)

Beneath the vote of confidence that the Commission gave to the modern world, one can discern some doubts. In several extended discussions, the members of the Commission expressed some confusion about the meaning and function of baptism and confirmation. Of course, the interpretation of these rites had concerned the Church for some time; the Commission had plenty of company in their confusion. I mention it here, therefore, only to suggest that beneath what appears to be the Church's confidence in the course of social change, there are some misgivings. How does the Church guarantee, for instance, that babies, once baptized, will grow up in the faith? Can godparents really be asked to speak "in the name of" a child or only "on behalf of" a child? What is the meaning of a profession of faith by proxy in a world that leaves open so many options even to the baptized? The Commission was especially concerned about the lack of "commitment" among adolescents. Since for every liturgical solution there were theological justifications and also theological criticisms, the Commission began to look to the bishops for further guidance. Finally, given the existence of services of baptism in other churches, there seemed to be no single "right way" to initiate infants as Christians.

The Commission was particularly divided over the question of whether baptism does or does not provide a decisive and complete moment in the initiation of the Christian. On one side were those who felt that the work of the Spirit in baptism could not be considered complete until the rite of confirmation has been administered; in confirmation the Spirit fulfills the person who appropriates the Church's faith at that time. On the other side were those who wished the moment of completion to be identified with baptism; after that the Church might have an interest in further testing the individual, but the work of the Spirit would have been done once and for all. The division produced a quiet entry in the minutes of the meeting in November 1966, which is worth quoting here:

"INTRODUCTION TO BAPTISM REPORT (Memorandum 72C)

Dr. Cuming introduced the memorandum and a general discussion followed, in which it was agreed that most of p. 1 should be rewritten. He later produced a draft which was substantially accepted, covering pp. 1 and 2, and making clear what are the two irreconcilable views of baptism involved in the service. At a suitable point on p. 3 the following revised footnote was to be inserted: 'The Rev. C. O. Buchanan would have desired the services more clearly to express that the work of the Spirit in the sacramental initiation is complete in baptism.' On p. 4 the paragraph on language was rewritten omitting reference to a modern-language appendix, and the following sentence was added at the end: 'Since the Rev. B. J. Wigan has been unable to attend many of the meetings concerned with the production of this Report, he would prefer not to be actively associated with the Report.'"

(Minutes of the Liturgical Commission, Nov. 1966, Item 87)

When the authority of the Church becomes secularized it is exceedingly difficult even for theologians and liturgists to find meaning in their several purposes no matter how many voices are included in a report or how many passages from Scripture are included as optional readings. Despite all these direct and indirect voices, the Commissioners could not agree on when, in a certain rite, a decisive moment has occurred completely and forever.

What seems clear from this brief introduction to the problem of revising a liturgical text for holy baptism is even clearer in the minutes of the Liturgical Commission's work on marriage. There is no need here to give exhaustive detail on the problem. Here too, multiple purposes are hardly framed in a single liturgical text. In a society that offers individuals many options, of course, it is not surprising to find individuals with many choices even regarding marriage, and the Church can reduce only a few of these options in designing its own rites. For instance, the minutes of the Liturgical Commission take account of new options for remarriage in a society more tolerant of divorce, and some on the Commission thought that in some cases "a second marriage was more Christian than the first" (Nov. 1966, Item 89). Where individuals have the option of marrying more than once, it is more difficult for the Church to attempt to reduce their options by insisting on the phrase "till death us do part"; that phrase, "though valuable, raised problems here" (Nov. 1966, Item 89). The secularization of the Church's authority becomes obvious when one member urges the Commission at this meeting to explore "both Christian and secular views," since the secular world offered insights and ideals of its own. Indeed, Mr Ayerst asked, "What did the Christian ideal add to the general consensus of opinion on what marriage should be?" (Nov. 1966, Item 89). Among other options, of course, are the rites and standards of other churches, and the Commission was well aware of these from the outset.

When the Church accepts and offers so many choices, it is difficult for an ecclesiastical rite to present even such a major step as marriage as a choice that ends all choices: a moment, once and for all, that completes and corrects all other moments in time.

Limiting One's Associations: The Sacred Context

The prime religious language of worship "is necessarily culture-bound" (Kolakowski 1982: 182). As Kolakowski reminds us, it may be futile to search for cultural universals in religion, for a core of religious meaning that can survive translation from one ethnic or linguistic community to another. It is particularly futile, according to the same argument, to separate faith from understanding, and understanding from membership in a concrete ethnic, historically contingent community. To search for texts that can mean the same thing to different people in diverse contexts is to seek a universality that negates the sacred by making it ordinary, mundane, uniform over many different occasions and contexts. Kolakowski is adamant on the point:

> "The language of the Sacred is not universal. This is to say that acts of worship do not retain their sacral sense in different civilizations; the words can be translated from one ethnic tongue to another, of course, yet not so their religious significance.
> ... people do not worship abstract concepts of hidden archetypes. They cannot extract from their religions a universal hardcore, common to all human races and cultures, and disregard all the historical forms whereby they express it. If there is such an essence, for instance in mystical experience, it is inexpressible either in words or in a ritual."
>
> (Kolakowski 1982: 181–82)

It is important to my argument that we appreciate the force of Kolakowski's assertion that religious myth and language "can only be understood within, as it were, through real participation in a religious community" (p. 176). Outside that context we find words used in a way that empties them of special meaning. They are plain as day, and they can be understood by those with little or no faith at all. Certainly some of those who are translating the Bible into modern English or revising traditional liturgies intend that the words speak with simplicity and plainness to a quasi-universal people whose primary qualification for understanding the words of faith is that they can read. Thus it is a paradox that liturgical revision should try to achieve a universal and plain language while at the same time insisting more rigorously on faith among those who would be married or baptized within the Church.

The community of faith tightens its organizational boundaries and at the same time weakens its symbolic boundaries by emptying its language of special and opaque meanings. That strategy, of course, is what one would expect in complex societies; less differentiated societies rely on strong symbolic markers and not on organizational boundaries. Consider Kolakowski's description of the language of worship; it fits ritualized, not secular societies:

> "the language of myth is closed or self-supporting. People become participants in this communication system through initiation or

conversion and not through a smooth transition and translation from the secular system of signs."

(Kolakowski 1982: 178)

The task of constructing liturgies requires the profound skepticism of the mystic who believes that, if silence must be broken, at the best one can manage only metaphors and negations. For the mystic one must say that God is like light, but then immediately deny that such a metaphor will do at all, since God is not likened to anything. Even the speech of glossolalia that claims to be the direct expression of divine messages requires translation and must therefore rank as one of the lesser gifts of the Spirit. But the liturgical commissions that put together the new books of worship held a profound distrust of all words as being, at best, mere communication tools, mere instruments. Theirs is the skepticism not of the mystic but of the modern individual who prefers effective action to words, words, words.

The Churches have been criticized for secularizing worship by reducing the sacredness of religious language in worship and by reducing the authoritative claims of religious speech (see Morris 1980). The critics argue that worship claims less authority when it is open to revision and permits only options for belief. Worship departs from the sacred when it tries to achieve a speech that transcends the context of the community of faith. Worship becomes a tool, a technique, a dispensable option: a strange and unsatisfying vehicle for speaking of the ultimate. Even where the Churches do claim to encompass the sacred, the Church's language offers so many options and alternatives that one can simply pick a myth-for-the-day. This is no way, I am arguing, for the sacred to lay claim to authority or to maintain the capacity of metaphors to enlarge literal, taken-for-granted notions.

A liturgy which is one of several alternatives hardly reminds the worshipper that life is a legacy, an inheritance, or that like grace, life is a gift. To provide alternatives within an alternative liturgy is to remind the worshipper that life is full of possibilities and that we are required to make many choices. But such a flexible and multi-purpose garment can hardly be put on with the same sense of being a grateful, even if unworthy, recipient as one has when donning the vestments, so to speak, of a worship that is preordained, inherited, and obligatory – *given*, and therefore to be accepted as it is, with humility as well as gratitude. Worship, if we are to follow certain parts of the old as well as new *Book of Common Prayer* is to remind us that "It is Thee who hath made us and not we ourselves." That reminder, I am suggesting, is carried most forcibly through a rite that we accept *in toto* or not at all: like the life that we have received from the hands of the Creator.

It is possible to find expressions of creaturely awe even in modern societies. In Arendt's (1978) appreciative discussion of "The Life of the Mind," she speaks of several modern poets who express a certain "admiring wonder" that Being has been given at all. They at least show how suggestive such affirmation can be as a solution for the apparent meaninglessness of an entirely secularized world. Here are two lines by the Russian Osip Mandelstam, written in 1918:

"We will remember in Lethe's cold waters
That earth for us has become worth a thousand heavens."

This verse can easily be matched by a number of lines by Rainer Maria Rilke in the Duino Elegies, written at about the same time:

"Earth, you darling, I will. Oh, believe me, you need Your spring times no longer to win me; a single one, Just one, is already more than my blood can endure. I've now been unspeakably yours for ages and ages. You were always right."

And finally, as a reminder, I cite again what W. H. Auden wrote some twenty years later:

"That singular command
I do not understand;
Bless what there is for being,
Which has to be obeyed, for
What else am I made for,
Agreeing or disagreeing?"
(Quoted in Arendt 1978: 185–86)

From the theological point of view, these lines, and Arendt's arguments, simply say that God "has not left himself without a witness" in the world, that creation is full of signs that evoke the testimony of the creature. But here, regardless of theological claims, language begins to convey what it represents, begins to evoke what it requires if it is to be understood. It is poetic language, and it does not lend itself, any more than worship, to sociological translations. Such language is far from the secular world of transient and revisable utterances, far from the world that is itself passing away. That secular world, as Mandelstam mentioned in the excerpt quoted above, is the land of Lethe, or death.

Conclusion

Ritual, like death, may wonderfully concentrate the mind when it offers only a single pair of options; for example life or death. If the larger society should offer only one competing vision, ritual can dramatize the decision placed before the believer as a choice between God and Caesar. In a society that offers its citizens many options, the choices offered by ritual will not so clearly contrast with those offered by the world. Try as it might to generate a clear-cut decision between itself and the world, any rite in a modern society will have difficulty in making the choice entirely clear to believers. Rituals that embody a number of options will place the believer not at a crossroads of faith so much as at the beginning of a labyrinth. When the believer leaves the ritual to "go forth" into "the world" it may not be entirely clear to anyone what is indeed at stake. This ambiguity is especially true, of course, of modern rites, especially some of the new versions I have mentioned, which offer a sometimes bewildering number of options themselves.

Less complex, less differentiated societies not only offer fewer options, they also rely more heavily on fixed and inflexible symbolic boundaries. Social authority in complex societies therefore employs flexible symbolic devices and revisable routines for separating various activities from one another; being complex and interdependent, such societies require more flexible and changeable notions of what is the right thing to do or the right time and place for doing things.

Where the community and the family clearly interpenetrate one another, it is especially important for symbolic boundaries to be clear, fixed, and inflexible. That is why the markers supplied in traditional rites were so very important: to distinguish the bride and the couple's property from what belongs to other households or to the community as a whole. Even in modern societies traditional rites still preserve this emphasis on essentially symbolic divisions: the exchange of vows, of rings, and of hand-clasps to signify the formation of a new unit within the larger community. Now, however, couples have a wider range of symbols by which to signify their unity, and these symbols are more optional, changeable, and personal in their significance. The words and gestures of couples getting married are now often the creation or the choice of the couples themselves, and the same couple may renew or revise what they have done in new rites devised for couples who wish to reaffirm or revise their initial wedding vows. The increasing separation of the family from the modern community allows families to have a degree of privacy and separate property ownership largely impossible in simpler, less differentiated societies.

More complex and differentiated societies rely more on organizational authority than on custom in employing symbolic markers to determine where people belong and when things will be done. In a modern office building movable partitions subdivide a large space for different actions that may go on simultaneously: play or recreation in one corner, where office-workers are eating or talking; a mixture of work and play near a coffee-maker; and varieties of work in a large number of cubicles. In these work-spaces some projects unceremoniously end as others begin. The individual worker makes many of the decisions about what to do next, except when contingencies arise and higher-ups issue new directives. Conversations follow patterns, but taking turns and shifting topics is relatively pragmatic and fluid. Of course, workers seldom initiate or terminate conversations without the tacit approval of their superiors, but the formalities are seldom explicitly observed.

The stages of life in a secular society also require a variety of flexible markers. The rites of passage vary from abandoning chastity and owning automobiles to becoming confirmed in a religious tradition or taking academic degrees. Who is to say with final authority when adulthood arrives in a modern society? Even maturity does not arrive at a certain time but becomes a lifelong project. We can still trace the patterns by which the young find mentors and the middle-aged train their successors, but the ages for promotion and for retirement vary, and the markers for each age shift in response to economic and political pressures. The transition from life to death also becomes a matter for careful analysis and legislation. New ideas and techniques have changed the popular and legal understanding of when death has occurred or new life begun. Modern societies do have markers for the stages of life, but like the partitions in an office building, the markers are quite flexible.

In relatively undifferentiated communities the same people regularly come together at the same time and at the same place for a variety of activities; for example, for planting, eating, dancing, love-making, and the choice of a new leader. Apportioning different activities to different times at the same place is essential to avoiding confusion over whether the time is right for sowing or dancing, loving or electing. In relatively simple societies, certain actions must finish before new ones can begin; actions, in other words, *must* become acts. Actions thus become complete when someone acknowledges the deed as done. In Church services we can still see a remnant of this process when congregations say "Amen" after the pastor utters a prayer. The action of the prayer only becomes complete when the Amen is done; the words only then are enacted, so to speak. In these less differentiated societies it is the same with promises and threats, planting and killing, harvesting and giving birth, growing up or growing old. These actions, whether they are words or deeds, are done only when someone, a priest or the people, says or sees that they are done. Parting is done properly only with a blessing, otherwise one leaves without permission or pardon. Until the action of parting is completed properly, moreover, one cannot go on satisfactorily to the next thing, and the next thing may not prosper. There is a beautiful description of just such an incomplete parting in Kelly's account of the kiss of peace that never took place between Thomas à Beckett and Henry II, with the result that Beckett parted unreconciled and therefore still in danger from his king:

"The King of the English had no sooner left Freteval than he came to his senses. He saw, in the course of a fever that presently overtook him, that he had conceded too much. As in other times of indecision, he took to restless journeyings. He wore out his following bustling from place to place, so that Thomas could not surprise him with demands for the kiss. Twice Thomas, who had been warned not to return to Britain without the guarantee, caught up with him. When other expedients failed, the archbishop sought to obtain the token by the ruse of standing next to the king at mass and offering him the pax. But Henry managed to have a requiem sung that day, so that no kiss should be required of the communicants."

(Kelly 1950: 145)

The proper rites separate in simpler societies what complex societies separate by organizational boundaries. Work or love-making, politicking and play may go on among the same people and in the same place in an undifferentiated society, so long as certain rites make possible the transition from one activity to the next. Rites point the way out of the labyrinth of possible words and deeds that are possible in a given place at any time. But in a modern society the substitution of separate places for work and play, for schooling and healing, provides organizational strategies for what simpler societies ritually joined in proper succession. It was once important to know the time and place for sowing and for harvest, for joy and for sorrow. It is now important to know what is the appropriate context for the range of human emotions that may come into play even in places ostensibly devoted only to one, such as work. The modern stranger is no longer the one outside the ceremonies of the community but one who does not know how to act appropriately. Of course, in these circumstances the symbolic markers that separate various activities will be flexible and temporary.

Rituals in less complex societies therefore accomplish more than the simple economy of assigning action to specific times and places. Some rites, as I have noted, also announce the beginning and end of things: the moments when what is said is also what has been done. These rites take actions and pronounce them done and make it unnecessary to say more on a given subject, since all the words necessary for the occasion, say for burial or for cooking, for planting or for cleaning, have been said. Nothing is left over; there is nothing more for the time being to be said or done. Actions and words combine to form what *is*. Actions become acts: part of the world that is and will be and cannot be undone.

Some actions, of course, even in primitive societies, are not finished until the last word is spoken, and some actions require more speaking than others; a death, for instance, is not done until there is nothing more on the subject to be said or done. Gluckman (1965) notes the ingenious techniques of divination and of trial that primitive societies even today will adopt to resolve what is otherwise unfinished at times of death. Did a kinsman die "naturally" or because of someone's ill will? Was that ill will conscious or unintended? Was the malicious feeling transmitted through magic or sorcery, through legitimate means or through foul? The dead person's soul, like the matter itself, will not rest until the last word is spoken. In an undifferentiated society ritual would disclose the presence, the source and intent of the magic, and when the rites are properly performed the community could lay to rest its grievances; various rites, from the wearing to the scattering of ashes, would enable the dead and the living to carry on. In a modern society, however, the autopsy is separate from the trial, and the trial is separate from the funeral. Because the last word is seldom spoken, a final inclusive judgment on the meaning of certain actions seldom given, societal pressure for a final test begins to accumulate. Such pressure can eventually shatter the containers of ritual and release hatred and a desire for revenge into everyday social life.

Like individuals whose work is never completely begun or ended and who turn night into day, a community without definitive acts will lack a clear identity. Nothing in such a community will be complete; and a community without the capacity to declare actions as completed will lack standards for perfection and judgment. All actions will be in progress, and the only sign of progress will be continuing activity. In a wholly secular society everything would be continuous but never done once and for all. Acts would disappear in a sea of actions that continuously pass away. That is why such a society, in its pure form, would be entirely secular; it is the quality of the secular always to be passing away. Early Christian theology considered a world of such continuous transience, a world so incomplete and lacking in standards of perfection, as to be headed for death.

5

The Passion to Act in the Public Realm: Across the Third Threshold

There is something Puritan about the search for the perfect act; certainly among those who have acted out the dream of the perfect act the Puritans rank among the most serious and persuaded. Carroll writes of the Puritans' emphases "on constant introspection, on self-scrutiny, on the individual being totally honest about himself, his acts and their motives – indeed, acts were to be judged in terms of their motives" (Carroll 1977: 4). It was difficult enough for the Puritan to cross the first threshold of action, so complex and devious were the motives that could underlie – or give the lie to – the best of intentions. Puritans were what Weber would call virtuoso: masters of the spirit – the emphasis here, of course, is on mastery, the desire for a pervasive control of all aspects of an individual's life. Just as God works His purposes out through the devious channels of human actions, so the spiritual virtuoso knows that there is no such thing as accident or mistake (see Carroll 1977: 6): "For the Puritan nothing is forgotten: a man's acts articulate his being, which is a coherent entity" (p. 5). Think for the moment of the Puritan as an individual in search of authority. That authority, of course, was a monopoly of the divine, but in this life one individual, if elect, and if one so chose, could turn his life into a text, an original text, whose every word served a purpose; despite the many chapters and the apparent multiplicity of purposes, they had one ultimate meaning: vocation, the working out of one's salvation in fear and trembling. After all, it was God, the author of all destiny, who inspired the earthly author to make of life a coherent and inspiring text. As Carroll puts it:

> "This character's stature was one of authority.... Believing that each man should accept full authorship of his acts, the Puritan lived as if he had full control over the configuration of his behavior, as if he should be praised for its virtue or blamed for its vice."
>
> (Carroll 1977: 8)

Here the key term is "as if": an element of make-believe inhered in the Puritan's search for the complete and perfect act; that is why I speak of that search as a "dream" that is acted out under the inspiration and guidance of religious culture. Even the Puritan knew the dream was impossible, so great is the weight of sin and ineradicable are the effects of guilt.

The strength of the Puritan dream, then, is partly in enabling the individual to cross the first threshold of action; the goal of purity of heart is upheld from the beginning even though it is considered hopeless apart from the grace of God. In aproaching the second threshold of action the Puritan dream seems more open to correction by others. For instance, it is incumbent upon the Puritan to act consistently according to purposes that share a common meaning even though they be apparently discrete; the Puritan is also energetic in building up a community in which disparate purposes can share a common meaning among those whose voices, at least, are heard and who attend to the same reports of voices in the Scriptures. The early New England communities attest to the strength of the social imperative in this stage of completing action into acts; the company of the faithful is a necessary, although not sufficient, condition that must be met if actions of one or more individuals are to be found faithful. In this sense, the Puritans extended to the believing community what the Catholic tradition asserted of the Church: outside its boundaries there is no salvation.

Within the community, however, salvation is not secure; actions may not be completed into incontrovertible and irreversible acts unless they have the capacity to combine private purpose and social meaning with public response; it is at this threshold, moreover, that the Puritan dream reaches a crisis. Carroll focuses on the doubt among early Puritans that the public sphere, where economic and political purposes come into play, can be anything more than a distraction or, perhaps at the most, an arena in which exemplary virtue is visible if not effective; his comments, however, extend not only to early Puritan communities but to the Puritan residues in the thought of such sociological divines as Max Weber:

> "In fact there is a series of contradictions within the Puritan persona, all amplifying the root absurdity that the individual spent his life atoning for his guilt under the hopeful illusion that redemption was possible, that truth would finally reveal itself.... When such a character manifested himself publicly, choosing an arena like the political in which to dispel some of his demons, his involvement was marked by deep seriousness, cautious evaluation, and yet, in spite of scrupulous rationality, the passion to choose and to act."
>
> (Carroll 1977: 9)

This public concern was not utopian or millennial; the Puritan was realistic about society as well as about character. The involvement was passionate, as Carroll points out, in contrast with the merely theatrical politics of celebrities or with the calculated rationality of experts in the public sphere. Weber's insistence that politics is a vocation is a final statement of this Puritan ethos; in it Weber did claim that the individual must take full responsibility for actions in the public sphere without expecting satisfactory results or public acclaim. As Carroll notes, such an ethos under the conditions of a highly complex society is moribund and, in Weber's case, crushing (Carroll 1977: 9ff.).

More has changed, however, than the social "environment." Granted that modern societies are "complex," the Puritan ethos is itself transformed into its opposite. The responsibility for salvation lay with the individual, the possibility with God: that was, crudely oversimplified, the Puritan credo. In certain contemporary authors, however, one can detect an inversion through which the responsibility for the lack of salvation or wholeness in human action lies with the larger society (or with particular social classes and institutions) while the possibility of wholeness resides with the individual. Take, for example, Quinney's lament:

> "The alienation experienced in labor becomes the condition for all areas of life. Ownership and control of life in general have been surrendered to alien hands. The production of life itself under capitalism has become alienated. Our lives as well as our productions are subverted and alienated in the historical context of capitalism."
>
> (Quinney 1980: 2)

There is no doubt here as to where the responsibility lies; it is with a capitalist social system – no doubt of that. The responsibility is a heavy one indeed, since it takes away the possibility of authority from the individual – the possible authorship of one's own life. No matter what purity of heart attends action and, furthermore, no matter what meaning can be construed from various individual purposes, the translation of these actions into acts that will command response or find fulfillment in contexts beyond the most immediate lies outside the scope of individual action. Deprived of authority, the individual blames the system.

"Blame" is a key element in the lament of the individual who finds the system alienating. No longer an alien because of a Christian pilgrimage that one can only take alone, toward a destination that lies forever beyond any social horizon and along a path emblazoned with marks visible only to the eyes of God, the individual blames alien-ness on the system; there lies the responsibility – in a society that is demonic because it deprives even the most authentic and meaningful actions of fulfillment and fruition. At least the Puritan found inward sources to blame for the war of all against all; the heart was full of warring impulses that could find expression in social life, and these impulses also set one individual in opposition to others. The responsibility for turning actions into acts lay with the individual, even if the possibility of authenticity, integration, and now of authority lies with God. It would be hard to find a more pointed comment on this inversion of responsibility than Carroll's:

> "In the paranoid we find a dichotomization of the private and the public similar to the Puritan's, but with reversed focus. The paranoid has lost confidence in private authority. He lives in fear of domination or threat from his environment, and he projects authority on to representatives of the public."
>
> (Carroll 1977: 12)

This comment is indeed pointed; it labels as "paranoid" the view that "true human nature ... is impossible under the conditions of capitalism" (Quinney 1980: 4). It was presumably possible under the conditions of national socialism, but that is a question I will take up shortly; the inversion of Puritan thought does see possibilities for redemption in modern societies, but they are located in classes with Messianic possibilities. Here the question is whether it is fair to label as "paranoid" the inverted Puritan argument that it is the world, and especially the world of modern societies, that stands in the way of humanity rather than the impurities of the heart and the obscurity of human purposes that impede the struggle for authority. The answer depends on whether one is talking about "reality" or "truth."

A "paranoid" view of modern societies is not difficult to support so long as one looks at social facts without asking the "truth question." The social facts of societies as large and complex as the largest capitalist nation-states are too well-known to need rehearsal here. The facts embody contradictions: unprecedented levels of prosperity and widespread poverty; high degrees of individual freedom and civil liberty alongside official secrecy, bureaucratic administration, and economic competition that leave many individuals relatively powerless to defend their own privacy and interests. The level of trust in public officials and major social institutions has declined steadily over the past twenty years in the United States, for reasons that inhere in the size and complexity of institutions as well as in unfair and oppressive practices in public administration. If such a view of modern societies is "paranoid," it is shared by a wide variety of social analysts both on the ideological Right and on the Left. What Lasch has called the "culture of narcissism" (Lasch 1980: 197) – namely, a general suspicion of appearances, of public officials and institutions, and of all social arrangements that purport to be caring or trustworthy – has its roots in competition and in the invasion of the world of family, friendship, and local community by the agencies of public power. One would be hard put to it to argue that anxiety, fear, and chronic feelings of helplessness and distrust do not have a basis in social reality.

It is the truth of such social arrangements that concerns the sociologist in the Durkheimian tradition, and the same concern animates Quinney's Marxist-sociological protest against a society that deprives individuals of their "true humanity." In relating Marxism and theology, in fact, Quinney reopens the question of the truth that is begged by discussions of social reality under specific historical circumstances:

> "Marxism and theology are confronting each other in ways that allow us to understand our existence and consider our essential (infinite) nature. Redemption is not only an historic phenomenon, but also a religious condition to be realized."
>
> (Quinney 1980: 5–6)

If one can only protest against one's inability to realize redemption in the context of one's own society, that is in itself a fundamentally

Protestant and – I would add – Puritan standpoint. Quinney does more than protest, however; he announces the possibility of redemption through religious socialism. The truth question can therefore not only be asked in a way that exposes the pathology of modern societies in general and capitalist ones in particular; it can be answered. That is what I mean by the inversion of the Puritan standpoint.

Before becoming more involved in a discussion of Puritanism, however, it may be well to consider what is at stake here. I am arguing that the religious hope for a complete and irreversible, incontrovertible social act is only a utopia or a fantasy under certain social conditions – particularly those of the modern nation-state in industrialized societies. Granted that no specific society offers a complete set of the conditions that are necessary for such a fulfillment; nonetheless, in the Durkheimian tradition the possibility is held out that individuals can realize their fundamental nature in society. That nature is social, and society can exhibit the aspects of "nature." There is such a thing as truth, and it is universal, however much or little a particular society's reality exhibits or distorts it. Durkheim was particularly critical of pragmatism's effort to beg the truth question precisely because, in adapting to a hypothetical social environment, individuals may well forfeit rather than fulfill their human nature. The same critique of society, focused on religion, underlies the Marxist polemic against religion. As Quinney rightly observes, however, Marx extended that criticism from religion to law and from theology to politics; secular societies are not exempt from the charge that they distort the truth no matter how compelling and coercive their reality (Quinney 1980: 6). One can become so lost in the data of modern societies that one fails to observe the social facts that these societies either exhibit, distort, or disguise. Durkheim as well as Marx would have approved of Quinney's assertion that:

> "Our humanity is not exhausted by our capacities for reason alone. Emancipation and redemption are joined in the fullness of our being ... The ultimate meaning of the substance and form of any culture transcends all the empirical realities of finite existence – although the signs of infinite reality are to be sought in the substance of human forms, and these forms are where the infinite is concretely realized."
>
> (Quinney 1980: 7–13)

A Puritan would profoundly agree, and with Quinney would speak of the divine providence that provides for social life in ways that transcend the capacity of even a keen empiricism to discern.

The sociologist's faith that society can take part in the realm of nature is a necessary antidote to the chronic fear and suspicion that attend the collapse of the Puritan dream. I agree with Carroll's argument on the fate of the Puritan ethos in the modern world; a Puritan without faith does become paranoid. The Puritan has the dream of completing action into acts by the grace of God; the paranoid knows that such action will never be fulfilled and will always be cut short by the authorities. Lacking faith in providence, the secularized Puritan becomes hopeless about the capacities for genuine autonomy and fulfillment in the modern world. Fully as convinced as the Puritan of the darkest impulses in the human heart, the paranoid finds that same darkness in others and especially in the institutions that purport to care and guide; "The Night is Dark and I am Far From Home" is the title of one criticism of educational institutions as heartless and deceptive, and the title is a particularly apt one since it comes from a Christian hymn that proclaims its faith in a God who does lead the pilgrim on (Kozol 1975). Without such faith, one can only attack those in authority who deprive the individual of the power to act authoritatively. No more likely than the Puritan to pursue sensual pleasures, the paranoid lacks the faith in a fulfillment that turns pleasure into joy; the alternative is a lifestyle that is neither pleasurable nor genuinely ascetic. As an antidote, then, to such skepticism, it is particularly important that the sociologist insist once more on the existence of a truth that cannot wholly be relativized. As Carroll puts it, "The relativist falsely assumes that the 'realist' in claiming an order of things takes that order to be absolute ... [But] the relativist's very denial of 'reality' is paranoid, disclosing a projection on to the realist of his own incapacity to think in non-absolute categories" (Carroll 1977: 14).

To put it very simply, the dream of acting in a way that achieves significance will never come true if the relativists are always right. To cross the third threshold, an actor will act in a way that produces a compatible and affirmative response; that response, furthermore, must come from those who were not the immediate recipients or audience of the initial speech, gestures, and deeds. It is only when actors find that they have been taken seriously by those who were the intended beneficiaries of their action that they know they have acted with some authority. That is, in crossing the third threshold actors gain authority as others, who are not immediately engaged with them in the small world of face-to-face encounters, take them at their word. That is what it means, for instance, to write a will; one acts in a way that requires the assent of one's intended beneficiaries who are not the immediate recipients or audience of one's words, gestures, and deeds. Only when the will is probated and put to the test is the action complete at this stage; it is then *significant*. Prior to that time, of course, the will might embody the individual's motives and intentions and have a meaning that encompasses a multiplicity of purposes, but it is still not significant until it is in effect. In a world where there is no grounding for speech that cannot be subverted by other speech, all such wills are relative and can easily be relativized. The paranoid view that I have just described, following Carroll's analysis, would appear to insist that no will can acquire such authority; the Puritan, despite all social appearances to the contrary, knows that there is a realm of law in which all meanings can be judged and some, at least, be probated successfully. That is, in fact, the Christian affirmation embodied in the Scripture; it is no accident that these writings are called a new "testament": not only a witness but a will, through whose reading and probation in the court of human experience the initial words, gestures, and deeds of the author will find their intended beneficiaries.

Early in this chapter, I suggested that the Puritan dream reaches a crisis at the third threshold. There the individual faces the resistance of social life to all actions that claim authority. It is the public sphere, with its own interests and rules, that presents an apparently insuperable barrier to individual action. The Puritan, I argued, seeks to control all aspects of life because in all these aspects the individual's actions become a text that bespeaks its author; to put it the other way around, the individual produces his or her own life as if it were a text, in which every word, gesture, or deed reflects on the author. In seeking to be the author of one's life, of course, the individual must come to terms with those whose purposes conflict with the individual's own purpose; the threshold of meaning must be crossed on the way to authority. The crisis, however, comes at the third threshold, where an individual's actions may not be considered authoritative by their intended beneficiaries.

A will may not be probated, just as a life may not pass the test of public opinion or be thrown out of the court of public interest. In adopting Carroll's portrait of the Puritan, I agreed that the Puritan's action was marked not only by "deep seriousness" (threshold one) and "cautious evaluation" (threshold two), but by "the passion to choose and to act" in the public realm (threshold three). There, however, lies the major impediment to the Puritan dream of completed action, since the public realm is often indifferent or resistant to the individual's will and has a will or wills of its own. There it may be apparently impossible for an individual to act with authority, but failure there puts an ineradicable question-mark over the significance of the individual's life. To be a full human being, to achieve (as Quinney argues) one's "true humanity," requires that one act in the public realm as the author of one's own life; otherwise one only reproduces another's order and obeys an order that estranges one from one's own life.

The third critical dividing line, then, between action that founders and action that makes its way toward a completed act is the boundary between the public and the private – an exceedingly difficult line to locate in the social world. The boundary is often merely analytical and represents a transition that is difficult at best to locate in specific instances. For instance, the boundary may stand for the distinction between political and familial contexts, or between the economy and the world of leisure; a few instances of élites appointing members of their families to high office or making important economic decisions in their social clubs are enough to suggest the difficulty of drawing such a line. The line is also difficult to draw because it is controversial; in a society where sexual activities reflect the domination of one gender by another or sports siphon off class hatred into symbolic contests, any effort to draw the line between public and private will be caught up in polemic. Not to ignore such controversy or the analytical difficulties of using this distinction, I would like to use the notion of a boundary between public and private aspects of social life in a rather limited way. Here the distinction simply refers to the difference between the immediate and the intended beneficiaries of social action: an expansion of social context in both time and space. I am using the term in a somewhat archaic sense of the public as the arena in which the individual publishes his or her own actions as significant acts, actions worthy of and requiring a response. The action is itself a signal for response, just as the reading of a will publishes that will and calls for response that will make the will effective. To be public in this sense is to publish; think of the meaning of the term "to publish glad tidings." The will embodied in the New Testament can become effective only when it is published to those who are its intended beneficiaries, no matter how far these beneficiaries are removed in time and space from the initial actions. A degenerate use of the term gives rise to the notion of a public as the object of publicity; the public becomes a series of audiences at which a message is beamed rather than a set of beneficiaries to whom a signal is given. When the only signal given is electronic, the only response may be mechanical or commercial – a highly limited response that does not make it possible for the initial actions to gain significance no matter how many or how few switch channels or order the proffered pamphlets and buttons of the promoters.

To make the notion of this third threshold even more specific, consider the shift in discourse that is required as one translates speech for the benefit of those who are not initially present. There are several steps that are required if the action is to be completed in the terms of a discourse in which it is not initially uttered, and I cannot begin to provide a complete list of them; I have ignored, for instance, the factors of dialect and language; obviously, few listen to the original New Testament message in Aramaic, and it is important to ask how much significance is lost in translation. Nonetheless, the following discussion will illustrate aspects of discourses that must be transcended or "translated"; remember simply that the third threshold is a passage from one "discourse" to another, and that certain aspects of discourse must therefore be bridged together.

One aspect of what I call discourse is a "topic." I have already mentioned that topics are what comprise a discourse, and that every context has certain rules for including or excluding particular topics. Politics and religion are frequently excluded, I suggest, not only because they are so often controversial but because they have become vehicles by which individuals press their claims for authority on one another. In a more complex society, of course, certain topics are reserved for experts; the Quinlan family, for instance, found it difficult to assert their claim in court to speak with some authority on the subject of their religion, and the question of whether or not their daughter, Karen Ann, could be considered "dead" or hopelessly and irreversibly comatose was reserved for doctors who were qualified to speak on such topics as "experts." Even the question of what their daughter had meant when she had expressed her feelings about the use of "heroic" measures to sustain life failed to carry weight in this latter context, so separate were the discourses appropriate to the family and the court. Quinney, as I have noted, attributes to complex societies the separation of one discourse from another that, as in the examples I have just given, makes it often a tragic surprise to individuals who claim the right to speak with authority; indeed, the purpose of the Quinlans' suit was to have the court uphold their word to their daughter, a word which they considered a virtual promise. No wonder that Quinney, quoting Tillich, argues that "this is symbolic of our whole civilization," namely, the shock of discovering that there is a void over which one's word cannot cross and that one's words, deeds, and actions are therefore so often, and so profoundly, insignificant (Quinney 1980: 8).

To agree on a topic is one of the ways in which actors find common meaning in their separate purposes; topics come into play, therefore, at the crossing of the second threshold and not only in connection with the third threshold where the distance from one discourse to another has to be traveled. I make this point because it is easy to confuse elements of discourse with discourse itself and so to minimize the scale of the problem. Much attention is devoted, for instance, to the study of what are sometimes called "practices"; that is, accounts that people give to one another to give meaning to their purposes. An account focuses on "the practices involved in providing for the world and displaying its rule-governed properties" (Silverman and Torode 1980: 172). In arguing over a topic, for instance, individuals may challenge the rights of one another to say what a particular controversy is "about"; at stake is a "practice," however, and not a "discourse." To return to an earlier example for a moment, consider the conversation of Emmaus: one speaker may say that what was really going on at the crucifixion of Jesus had to do with an aborted revolution, while another says that the proper topic here is not revolutionary strategy but the witness of the Old Testament prophets. The discourse is the same, for reasons that will become clearer as I proceed with a list of the elements of discourse; certainly the context only concerns the immediate recipients and audience of the the actors involved. The accounts or practices, however, vary from the distraught disciples to the stranger they meet on the road to Emmaus; they vary in the way they seek to adapt to the situation (vary "in providing for the world") and in finding order in apparent chaos (vary in "displaying its rule-governed properties"). Of course, there is conflict here over whose voices are heard and what meaning is found to integrate apparently disparate purposes;

the discourse, however, remains intact. The individuals interpret, interrupt, and reinterpret one another in various power-plays familiar to all who engage in strenuous conversation; these practices are often the object of minute analysis by sociolinguists (see Silverman and Torode 1980: 17). Where topics are parts of separate discourses, however, it is not sufficient to engage in conversation over what "apparently" or "really" went on, say, at the crucifixion; no mere interruption and reinterpretation will be sufficient to bridge the gap. When two discourses are separate, as indeed they were in the case of Karen Ann Quinlan, to which I have just referred, what is at stake is the authority of the individual even to speak on a specific topic. The only way to bridge the gap between the discourse of the family (in which the parents had plenty of authority to make promises to their daughter on the subject of her possible medical care in extreme and tragic circumstances) and the discourse of the medical school, was to go to court in search of a signal that would grant significance to the parents' prior promises.

Ritual of course is a means of bridging the gap between dis-courses. Christian ritual, for instance, typically provides a signal by which to translate one discourse into another. There is little oppor-tunity in the liturgy for individuals to interrupt and reinterpret one another's discussion of particular topics; even the sermon, which focuses on topics relevant to everyday life, is not easily interrupted, although it seeks to reinterpret commonsense understandings into a framework that explains what "really" going on. The rites of the Churches simply make public the purposes and meanings of individuals in a variety of words, gestures, and deeds on a wide variety of topics; take any list of intercessions, for example, and one will find the topics on which individuals are thus publicly expressing themselves for the benefit of those who are not then and there present. That is precisely the point of intercessions: that they shall be made effective in a later time and place on occasions provided for by a divine providence.

To pick one other aspect of discourse that further illustrates what I mean by that term, I wish to include "ways of speaking." Here again is a familiar phrase to students of sociolinguistics, and I give it a specific meaning in this discussion that is compatible with the usage of some of those discussions. By a "way of speaking" I mean prac-tices for addressing people and problems. People, of course, may be addressed by names or by titles: by references to their personal qualities or by references to their relevant place in the group or the community. Problems may also be addressed in ways that make sense primarily to those most immediately concerned or in ways that might well be intelligible or helpful to people who are not presently concerned at all. These ways of speaking are sometimes called "codes" or "registers" (see Bernstein 1972), and the discussion is often further confused by controversial argument over what constitutes "competence" (see Silverman and Torode 1980: 171–99). The point of the controversy over "competence" is that certain ways of speaking may well be more effective in bridging the gap between two kinds of discourse than other ways of speaking. The discourse of the home may be compatible with that of the school or the court when those in authority in the latter institutions are also parents of children who, by learning certain ways of speaking, get a head start in expressing themselves in ways that are suitable in public. Of course, those who learn the approved ways of speaking are more likely to be able to speak with authority in the courtroom.

Controversies aside, the point I wish to make concerns the gap between discourses, and it is especially a gap between public and private discourse that concerns me here. Any kind of discourse (e.g. that of professionals or of everyday life) may have many ways of speaking. In conversation professionals may salt their formal arguments with anecdotes, and in everyday life individuals may pepper their stories with grandiose theories about human nature. More specifically, individuals may engage in preaching or persuasion at the corner store, and in their sermons preachers may in fact engage in gossip or chat. The presence of different ways of speaking in the same discourse leads to double meanings and to irony: in fact, the mixture of professional and commonplace ways of speaking pays a compliment to those who are speaking together, that they somehow know two things: what everybody knows and what the specialists know. Within a common discourse, then, the benefit of the doubt goes to those who are speaking with one another; not so, however, when one discourse confronts another. As I have already noted in the illustration of the Quinlan case, one discourse may claim a monopoly on professional ways of speaking and reduce the other discourse to the practice of everyday speech and of commonplaces; the same conflict between discourses may polarize speech so that only literal rather than ironic meanings and *double entendres* are permitted. Under these conditions, I am arguing, conflict between discourses awaits a resolution in the form of a signal; in the case of the court, for example, that signal is given in the form of an opinion, a verdict, or a sentence.

There is another aspect of discourse that comes into play whenever a gap emerges, say, between public and private speech. Any discourse embodies what Halliday calls "a complex of acts in some ordered configuration" (Halliday 1978: 142–43). Although speaking of a "situation," Halliday's comments serve to summarize what I have already included in describing discourse and to introduce an additional element. I have mentioned the topic (what Halliday might call subject-matter and a text) and also ways of addressing particular people and problems (what Halliday calls a role structure for speech). Some of these roles pertain to the immediate situation and some borrow from the larger society. In the case of a baptism, for instance, parents and children are present in both sets of roles, as parents and children (roles borrowed from the larger society) and as persons to be baptized or to sponsor candidates for baptism. All of this structure would not be possible, however, if it were not for an agreement on priorities. By this I mean the right to speak first or second – priorities in speech. I also mean, however, the priority of one role-set over another: on whether one's status as child or parent has priority over one's status as someone seeking baptism. A third priority governs the relation of speakers to the topic: the right to choose the text, for example, whether the text is a Scripture reading, a document submitted in court, or the report of a conversation. The agreements on the right to speak and on the priority of various roles will affect and perhaps govern the agreement over topic and text. Where priorities are well ordered there is ample room in discourse for subtlety, irony, the play of *double entendres* and conflicting interests, and for interpretation, interruption, and reinterpretation. Between discourses, however, the agreement over priorities is precisely what is at issue, and only the simplest and most literal meaning can be the object of agreement.

What one discourse gives the highest priority, of course, may be of relatively low priority in another; there is the rub between ends and means and between the sacred and the secular. In crossing the second threshold, action arrives at a symbol that unites multiple purposes: a flag, a cross, a handshake or a signature. In passing over the third threshold, however, these symbols diverge or come into conflict with one another and with other signals: the flag conflicts with the cross; a handshake becomes insignificant and only a signature will complete a contract when discourses become separated. Earlier in this book I mentioned Parsons's concern with action that must come to grips with the fact that one person's ends are another's means (see O'Neill 1982: 103). What one person has pursued as an end (devotion to God) may be to another merely a means (a way of attaining peace of mind); the promise of the Quinlans to their daughter, clearly an end in itself, becomes merely a bit of data to the court. The resolution of discrepancies and conflicts between discourse therefore requires something more than a symbol; it requires, I am arguing, a signal in which the element of command is explicit. Only a signal, embodied perhaps in a gesture or a word as well as in a deed, can transcend the distance between discourses; to be significant, however, such a signal requires a corresponding and affirmative response.

Consider a hypothetical society in which discourses are incompatible – potentially and sometimes actually in conflict. Unlike societies in which ritual provides a signal to resolve conflicts between discourses, however, this society is impoverished in ritual. The significance of words, gestures, and deeds is largely undertermined, although the culture requires each individual to assess the significance of his or her own as well as of others' gestures in order to give the right response. An ethic of responsibility is basic to that society, but ways of acting responsibly are left to the individual until a conflict requires adjudication. To paraphrase Carroll's discussion of modern culture, I would suggest that such a society is Puritan in its insistence on responsibility and paranoid in its inability to assess the significance of specific actions.

I call this society "hypothetical" because it exists only as an extrapolation of specific features of Western societies, and specifically of the United States, that have institutionalized and secularized a Puritan culture. In the following pages I will suggest how pervasively that culture still affects everyday life in English-speaking societies. I will point out how Puritan residues lead individuals to experience life as a continual testing, an incipient trial, and as a process of waiting for an authoritative signal that will end disputes over conflicting priorities. I will also point out how a secularization of these societies leads individuals to no permanent conclusions about priorities and no resolution, therefore, of debates over individual and social responsibility. That process of secularization is specifically evident in the separation of private from public discourses and in the restriction of sacred discourse to the private sphere. Only when individuals seek to speak publicly and with significance on matters they hold sacred do the two discourses come visibly into conflict and require a signal that will resolve their conflicting priority.

To summarize, the Puritan dream of actions completed into acts has always suffered a crisis when it meets the resistance of the public sphere to the authority of individual purposes. Not only do these purposes require affirmation within a community, but the community that finds meaning in them may not be able to act on that meaning in the public sphere of politics and economics. Initially the resistance of "the world" did not dismay the Puritan, who found that persistence or – at the most extreme – withdrawal to another community would make it possible for the individual to work on his or her salvation even in the public sphere; only the end result was in doubt, and no public affirmation would relieve the Puritan conscience entirely on that score.

The Puritan dream of actions completed into acts has reached a more severe crisis in modern societies, however, as public discourse has become increasingly separate from private speech. I have mentioned three aspects of discourse that have become increasingly separate: topics, ways of addressing people and problems, and the assignment of roles to speakers in particular contexts. The separation of religion from other topics of public discourse occasionally breaks down, in periods of crisis, of political mobilization during presidential campaigns, and when specific issues of religious freedom conflict with existing policies or practice. Attention to these more dramatic occasions, however, obscures the extent to which the most complex societies, at least in the West, have separated the topics of public policy from those of religion. It is simply unusual to have religious beliefs discussed in connection with the budget; only when specific items, like aid to religious schools, or various birth-control policies that include abortion, are being discussed, does religion enter into the on-going and routine discussion of public issues. This separation is further enhanced by a divorce between the ways individuals address political or technical problems and the way they address religious questions. Appeals to technical rationality prevail in the former, whereas in relation to religious questions rationality may be either highly instrumental (focusing on how religion "works") or highly substantive (focusing on the question of what is indeed either true or good). The ways that individuals address God have changed in the new Anglican and Episcopal rites to include "You" as well as "Thee," but the effort to close the gap between religious and secular discourse may not have succeeded in any more fundamental respect. This is not to say that bishops will not address themselves to public issues, but that politicians and administrators may be far less inclined to address ecclesiastical authorities on these issues: a major change from the time when, as Quinney noted, the minister and the magistrate were both public officials preoccupied with the community's entire welfare (Quinney 1980). Under these conditions, furthermore, it will be difficult for individuals in the public sphere to agree on who or what to take into consideration – to agree on priorities in speaking or on the topic or text to be considered. The Mayor of New York cannot tell the Archbishop of New York how to treat homosexuals employed by Catholic institutions – so rule the courts in that jurisdiction. In Washington Catholic universities may find that the magistrates do have a voice in such matters that they lack in New York. There is little agreement over who has the right to speak with authority on specific topics or on what topics should indeed have priority in the shaping of public policy. It is no wonder, given such anarchy, that the individual may find it difficult to be the author of his or her own life by speaking with authority in the public realm.

The Pursuit of Individual Authority: Ritual in a Secular Society

The Puritans at least succeeded in institutionalizing the notion of a last judgment in secular as well as in religious culture. Of course, the eschatology of the sects still proclaims the imminent return of the one who will judge the world and redeem his own people. That expectation places each society under continuous judgment and the individual believer on trial at every moment, lest the judge return and find his people distracted and unready – a Puritan's view of responsibility without any modern inversion. In the Churches with sacramental traditions the liturgy re-enacts the continuing return of the judge in a mock trial. In the liturgy the believer attends the rehearsal of the law, the re-enactment of judgment and absolution, and release on probation with the additional promise of divine strength and comfort. The responsibility for salvation still rests on the individual, the possibility rests still on God. Popular piety looks upon daily life as a continual testing in the face of temptation and suffering. But beyond these important differences among forms of religious culture, the secular world itself carries the residue of that eschatological expectation. It could not be otherwise, of course, in societies that have acquired their basic values and rules from religious culture, even though secular institutions now are independent and self-sustaining. Secular social authority still derives from the adoption of roles, governed by the values of rationality and responsibility, that now require only a *partial* correction and completion of the ordinary individual. In good times such partial transformations may be sufficient. In times when grievances and misgivings increase doubts about all social authority, however, pressures for a public accounting may make all authority very precarious.

This secularized, formerly Puritan ethic in Western societies derives in part from the eschatological fervor of biblical religion. The parables of the New Testament, now widely regarded as injunctions on life in the face of imminent and final judgment, constantly call upon the believer to make the most efficient use of whatever means are available without losing sight of the end. The very imminence of the end of history reinforces the claim on the believer to make the best use of time and talents in unceasing labour. The same eschatological push reinforces the drive toward responsibility in biblical expectation. The limited time remaining before the end makes each appeal of stranger and neighbor ultimately serious; not to respond to such immediate demands may result in being found wanting in the final judgment. Such, of course, is the message of the parable of the sheep and goats. Henceforth it is unforgivable not to know with whom we are dealing in the voices of the sick and hungry, poor or imprisoned. They are the advance notices of the judge who is finally coming. Even the doctrine of the eventual and second coming of the judge is taken in recent theology to reinforce the meaning of such eschatological parables that the coming of the judge is immediate, continuous, and ubiquitous: now and everywhere, in every sphere of human activity, from now on. There is no stronger theological support for the values of rationality and responsibility, whether or not such support is still needed. *Americans and other Western societies, I will argue, still hold the individual responsible; more responsible, perhaps, than under a theocratic regime, but responsible – I would add – for less and less. The incorporation of modern societies has drastically limited the liability as well as the authority of the individual.*

It is the West, of course, that found a way to place individuals on a perennial and unending trial in virtually every aspect of social life; rationality and responsibility become the alternative to genuine transformation. The Calvinistic view was simply that one was on trial for one's life before the throne of God's judgment; transformations would be postponed pending final judgment. The more orthodox viewpoint insisted that judgment had already been given, while a more heterodox Calvinism suggested that while the verdict had already been given in the crucifixion, the resurrection left open the possibility that sentence might be suspended for those who gave evidence in their lifetime of appropriate contrition, faith, and amendment of life. Even for Catholics, as one commentator on Tocqueville puts it, there is a "trial of faith"; one's life is perpetually on trial before an all-powerful and potentially merciful but invisible judge. The meaning of being "tested" or "on trial" has symbolized the meeting-place of individuals' many and sometimes conflicting purposes.

As each class has emerged from the peasantry or the proletariat to claim a measure of secular authority, they have faced the standards that apply, since the Reformation, to the priesthood of all believers: a certain sobriety, discipline, and authenticity that wed the person to the role of citizen in a moral republic. To cross the second threshold of action, the individual had to accept the obligation of being "on trial." However, where secular authority claims no sacred basis and requires no transformation of the person into an incumbent of a role or office, the trial of faith degenerates into a social process of testing; the individual is therefore born into a Kafkaesque world where one's entire life may be under surveillance and one's words or deeds cited as evidence. But the trial itself is only foreshadowed and never materializes in one's own lifetime. Faced with a complex world, the individual still acts as if his options were drastically limited by an implicit choice between salvation and damnation. Coles, in his interpretation of the working-class ethic of responsibility, notes:

> "We're here to be tested, like the priest says. It's a trial. You do the best you can. We're lucky to be in America. Think of how bad it is in other countries. I tell my children that in this life you have to do the best you can – work hard, bring up your children to believe in God and love their country and be good citizens, and obey the law ... That's what it means to be grown-up; you don't feel sorry for yourself all the time, and you don't go asking a lot from others,

and you don't expect the world to be served you on a silver platter, and like the priest says, you know the difference between Heaven and Earth."

(Quoted in Erikson 1978: 223)

The Enlightenment offered the West the same continuous and unending trial on secular terms. On the terms offered by the Enlightenment, modern societies could conduct business and politics, without the constraints and interferences of religion, as separate compartments. The separation of discourses was the price to be paid for religious freedom. Without religious interference in business and politics, modern societies could look forward to new freedoms, not the least of which was the freedom from religious vitriol in public life. There would be no more murder in the name of God. As a precondition for this freedom, however, the Enlightenment could still require that one conduct all aspects of personal and social life as though one were in fact on trial. In science one would assume that nature is orderly and therefore examine the testimony of scientific observers for distortions, omissions, and contradictions. The same judicial scrutiny of testimony sets the rules for all academic discourse; no speaker is considered credible who refuses to testify according to stringent rules concerning evidence. In a highly differentiated society each profession of course develops its own rules regarding expert and lay testimony, medicine and the law reserving for the professionally elect the right to pass judgment on their clients' descriptions of their symptoms or injuries. In each institutional sector, however, separate rules of discourse subject all testimony to examination for omissions and distortions. The individual can cross the third threshold of action in only one discourse at a time.

The rules for evidence are remarkably similar, as are the constraints on testimony, across the board from the law and medicine, to the classroom and to the therapeutic relationship itself. The most severe requirements for claims to authoritative and credible speech are no longer to be found in the confessional booth or the liturgy but in the secular hearings conducted by administrators and managers, as well as by teachers, lawyers, and doctors. The trial procedure, once limited to the Church and the state, now goes on under its own momentum in every authoritatively organized department of social life.

The separation of public from private discourse in a complex society makes it difficult for sacred authority to pinpoint responsibility and to make judgments and invidious comparisons. Complexity itself places many layers of organization between those who make policy and those who carry it out. Policemen on a beat or telephone operators, for instance, have their own jurisdictions and can affect people's lives profoundly, but usually make no claims to priority outside of these contexts. The same complexity gives most individuals a large number of options, so that they need not feel their lives summed up and their existence on trial according to how they conduct themselves in particular roles. The same argument applies even to roles within Churches and other religious organizations. This flexibility, however, ultimately deprives the individual of a forum in which to speak with authority in the public sphere.

In a secular society, only a slight transformation is necessary to empower individuals to act in their separate roles. What major transformation or achievement of character is necessary to empower a secretary to put someone "on hold" or a bank officer to deny someone credit? Officers, case workers, agents – these are roles that permit the individual to carry out policy or to control others without profound commitment or inner conviction. There is no opportunity or need here for the individual to acquire *personal* authority. Any individual can use such roles to express such impulses or to keep others away without becoming fused with the role itself. No transformation is required for actions such as these, no matter how fateful they may be for individuals left without credit, communication, or power. With so little call for hope and faith, for sacrifice and commitment on the part of those who exercise the petty authorities of modern societies, there is apparently little need for the rites of transformation

Given the separate principalities and powers of specific jobs and particular companies, few individuals can claim to be a part that embodies the whole organization. There is litle social use for transformation through a ritual that would enable a person to be so recognized and acclaimed. Policies, statements, decisions, procedures can all be reviewed and revised at higher organizational levels – hardly a situation that calls for the fusion of person with a role in a solemn rite or the achievement of a character that speaks with authority.

In a secular society, even roles in religious organizations call for little in the way of transformation and appear instead as a reward or opportunity for which individuals have a right to compete.

Conversely, the satisfactions of churchly roles may have become inadequate, or the penalties for abandoning certain strategic roles may have proven to be too weak, as in the large-scale defections of parish clergy during the last two decades. When the roles of the laity attract too few lay persons, attendance also declines, relatively few parents present their children for baptism or confirmation, and the confirmed lapse from their adult roles within the Church. Many laity may have too many more attractive options to undertake roles in the Church, while those with few alternatives may hang on to what roles they in fact possess.

To elect and appoint public officials, to ordain the clergy and license lawyers or doctors, to promote or hire professors are obvious examples of the direct exercise of social authority, but authority inheres only in policies that define the requirements by which individuals can become eligible to take roles. Even when individuals are found unworthy to continue in certain roles or the requirements for occupancy are contracted so as to eliminate entire classes of persons, authority inheres in an abstraction rather than in the character of those who pass such judgment.

A secular society can create new roles, determine their requirements, train and recruit individuals to occupy them, set limits on the roles, provide rewards for adequate performance, and determine when final departure from such roles can be called for. Hiring and firing, educating and retiring, planning and administering, creating and dissolving are work that presume authority, but in a secular society the face of that authority never appears except, perhaps, in the abstract guise of requirements for certification or for civil service. Kafka was right.

Secular societies place individuals on trial only as incumbents of a limited role in which individuals merely perform and say their lines. For the actors themselves, to take such a role is less of a risk and does not require the individual to cross the first threshold of action. The presence of many options allows the individual to be justified quite apart from particular performances. It is therefore less necessary for others in the drama and for the audience itself to have faith in the actors. One's associates need not believe in what they cannot see; that is, the actor's motives and sincerity, commitment and understanding. Merely competent performances in the roles themselves will suffice.

Some authority is necessary for the construction of roles and for the assignment of parts to particular individuals, but specific performances are a mock trial in which nothing serious appears to be happening. The need for rituals in secular societies is therefore hardly apparent. In simpler societies, of course, progress depended on the individual meeting critical tests of courage and endurance, and these tests were also critical for the individual's own sense of worth and immortality. Tests of prowess in the hunt examined the individual's willingness to risk death in order to provide the sources of life to the human community; they also enabled the individual to overcome the fear of death. So it was with tests of prowess in battle, in leadership, in mating. Simpler societies also prescribed ritual at the end of life itself, where spiritual strength guaranteed the right of the individual to make the last step in the company of the community's ancestors. The last rites posed the final question concerning the individual's motives and intentions – and also concerning the social meaning of a person's purpose in life.

Of course, charismatic claims may disrupt even a secular society. Spirited individuals may seek to reshape trivial or boring roles or to create new ones. Individuals certain of their inspiration may demand new recognition as the rightful incumbents of particular roles. Even in religious organizations the laity may question the clergy's right to a monopoly of religious roles, especially when the clergy appear to be apostate or simply unbelieving, whereas the laity may be speaking in tongues, receiving revelations, and offering themselves as a living sacrifice to be made holy by the Church's authority. Under these conditions women understandably seek ordination, and the young seek recognition in the governance and the liturgy of the Church. Similarly, the inspired seek a role in propounding the meaning of the Scriptures or in interpreting the utterances of the Holy Spirit. Charismatic claims make it both more difficult and more necessary for individuals to cross the second threshold of action.

The laity are acquiring more roles but not more authority. The clergy may give the laity more roles within the liturgy, such as reading the Scripture and distributing the consecrated elements, while gutting the sacramental powers of the laity to share the *production* of the sacrament itself. While the laity obtain more roles in the distribution of the symbolic products of the Church in word and sacrament, the clergy keep their monopoly over the actual production of the word and sacraments. Liturgical changes may therefore appear to bring the faith of the laity and the authority of the Church into closer harmony around new texts. But the introduction of the new texts actually reinforces the authority of the clergy over the laity. Demands for reform may thus lead to the perpetuation of the old order under new rules and forms: an observation that applies to civil rights movements or to student protest as well as to religious groups and movements. In this event, individuals may have more to do (i.e. more responsibilities), but less authority and even less public liability.

Compare, for example, the priest and the President as examples of individuals who, once transformed, enjoy uncommon authority: the one sacred, the other secular. To accomplish this transformation, this fusion of person with role, requires the services of ritual. No ordinary ritual suffices to shift from the ordinand to the priest or from the candidate to the President. The people must be present, cast their votes or voice their approval. The people must be consenting adults: not only lucid, informed, rational but in agreement on the priorities for letting specific individuals speak on particular topics in the public sphere. The authority of the priest is largely to demonstrate, show forth, and exemplify that for which the priest stands. The Churches may differ on what they think the priest stands for, but the point is the same. Transformation through ordination results in the formation of someone who at all times and places represents the faith of the Church: the person can be trusted to unite private with public discourse. The President enjoys a somewhat greater separation between the person and the office, because the President only engages in presidential acts at specific times and places, whereas the priest, as Simmel once put it, is a part indistinguishable from the whole, a piece of the Church that exemplifies and stands for the Church as a whole. The priestly transformation creates one who ideally will act in harmony with the role at all times and in all places; that is the priest's vow. The transformation of the presidential candidate creates an authority more powerful than the priest's but more limited to certain acts.

In American society, and I suspect elsewhere in the English-speaking world, priests, presidents, and prime ministers must confront a growing public conviction that "mere rituals" are empty, ineffective, and largely for "show." To consider a ritual as an empty ceremony suggests that any transformation is pretended or merely temporary. In the meantime, a Kafkaesque world emerges in which people perform their roles either tongue-in-cheek or with a certain seriousness and solemnity, although the face of ultimate authority never appears. Individuals, like Joseph K. in Kafka's *The Trial,* remain forever in a process of continuous testing in which the end, the promised day in court, never occurs; there is no revelation or final judgment. Like Joseph K. one is always preparing for something big in a process that never becomes complete, but as a result the individual remains in a state of continuous suspense or of arrested development (under arrest; see Fromm 1957, Ch.7.5). Social authority therefore becomes exceedingly problematical when any society gives only partial and temporary transformations. In a society with repeated elections, for instance, the candidate is always re-emerging from the President (the person, so to speak, from the role). It is difficult to be sure when the President is being the President or merely acting presidential. Perhaps the transformation is temporary because soon after election the President begins to act with an eye to re-election, and the white swan of the Oval Office becomes more like the ugly duckling on the campaign once again. Even rituals of ordination fail to leave the classic, indelible mark on the Catholic priesthood. No transformation lasts for long in a secular society. That is precisely why it is secular – transient and fated to pass away.

Complex societies make it particularly difficult for ritual to be a rite of passage at the third threshold of action. To be effective at that level, ritual must conflate private with public ways of speaking. One way of speaking (call it a "code") focuses on the person; the other code focuses on the position that person occupies in a community, say, or in a family (see Bernstein, 1974: 134 ff.). Modes of address indicate which code is being used: Mr Smith, Dr Jakowski, Jane, or Richard. The use of titles or names implies what is salient in the exchange and what degrees of equality or intimacy can be assumed. What matters may be a person's position in an organization or profession; or something far less authoritative and more personal may be called for. The use of a particular code provides one clue to the expectations in the classroom or office, in the agency or in the playroom. Some individuals may be pulling rank while others are demanding to be treated as equal in a situation; the codes in use do not always match. Indeed, when there is an opportunity for confusion as to which code is appropriate or obligatory, the door is open to disappointment and suspicion. Whether a person is engaging in an ethnic slur or being simply familiar; whether someone is being friendly or deliberately withholding professional recognition: these possible misunderstandings are two fairly obvious examples of a confusion of codes. If the individuals are to be trusted and taken at their word, (i.e. to speak with authority) the door to such confusion must be closed. To prevent or overcome mistrust it is necessary to adopt a way of speaking that creates agreement on how to address persons and problems and sets priorities on which roles of a person actually matter and will come into play in a particular context. To set these priorities and establish agreement on ways of speaking is one task of ritual. My point is simply that, under the aegis of ritual, two divergent and sometimes conflicting codes for locating or creating authority (one calling for personal, the other for positional responses) are brought closely together.

When ritual fails, individuals begin to forget, abuse or go outside the authority of their positions. Eventually pressures mount for a day of reckoning either in court or in the street; other pressures mount for a release from the constant burdens of being confined by a role and its responsibilities. In either event these pressures call for a day of fulfillment or reckoning.

The maintenance of social authority requires the management of respect and disrespect, of loyalty and disloyalty, of satisfaction and grievance. Rituals, in simpler societies, have been effective in reducing options and in focusing loyalties, in mobilizing respect for the incumbents of roles and in gathering the support of an entire community or society. Under the auspices of effective ritual one generation or regime succeeds another, and one stage of life yields to the next. Without ritual's auspices all new undertakings are taken with only questionable authority. In this chapter I have noted that rituals, by ensuring a certain transformation of a person into the rightful incumbent of a role, fuse the kinds of discourse in which people convey their regards to persons and to social positions and so ensure the person's authority in the role as well as the authority of the role over the purely personal interests of the individual. What ritual accomplished in simpler societies has only partially been carried forward, in more complex societies, by the values derived from Western religious tradition. Even in a complex society, I have suggested, individuals have understood themselves to be on trial and faced with a limited set of options within the constraints of an ethic of rationality and responsibility, but their authority and liability are exceedingly limited.

From one theological viewpoint, to make the trial the basis of social authority is asking for trouble. The story of the Garden of Eden also defines the human condition as one of trial set in an *apparently* benign environment. The representatives of the human race are under constant surveillance. The fruits of the trees are largely available for their nourishment, but one at least is prohibited. The conversation with the serpent is apparently harmless, since the serpent's intent is simply to clarify the meaning and intention of the divine constitution, a process in which academics and judges as well as the laity have been engaging for years. No crime has yet been committed, but every word, every gesture provides information that will later be used as evidence of worthy or unworthy intent by Adam and Eve. The deed done, the trial begins with a searching question to mankind: "Where are you?" It continues with cross-examination in an effort to assign responsibility for the betrayal of the divine confidence. If that responsibility is found to be shared by all of humanity, it is because all humanity has contributed to the betrayal.

The failing, theologically speaking, was to place God on trial by reviewing His original rules and testimony; that is a fundamental and personal flaw in the human condition. The verdict is simple enough. When humans place God on trial in their hearts, their own trial begins in earnest. In their banishment from Paradise, so to speak, humankind receives a continuance in its trial. There will be further hearings, with more evidence, plea bargaining, and judicial review. It seems, indeed, as if the trial will never end. Individuals in secular societies may have developed considerable tolerance for a lifetime of continual testing. Certainly the American – and perhaps the British – public has developed a tolerance for a society in which individuals are only partly trustworthy and have limited authority. If the only opposition to secular authority were from those religious groups that still demand total transformations in history, at least from pivotal figures and their followings, no warning would be needed; a simple caution about underestimating religious fervor in politics would be enough. It is the persistence of the myth of a Messianic people or nation, a myth without a clear embodiment in the Church and therefore without the limitations as well as the force of a political metaphor, that underlies the note of warning in the next chapter. Without rituals to express and also to contain the myth, the hope for transformation may have no bounds and may lead to political excesses for which there is no remedy.

6

The Fourth Threshold: Institutionalizing the Principle of the Will

"What has not been attempted is some stark encounter with the realities of power and political process. Reinhold Niebuhr, in the inter-war period, produced a highly sophisticated political theology, which took a left-wing position as its starting point, but eventually provided the basis for a kind of Christian realism, whether of Right or Left. The neglect of Niebuhr in the last two decades is symptomatic of a general softening of Christian political thought."

"Nothing whatever is guaranteed if we obey God's law. God does not underwrite his Kingdom in political terms. What we are here concerned with is not whether a righteous few might bring forth fruit after the collapse of those democratic polities on which we place so great a value, but with political responsibility, and we cannot off-load it onto the very long run of the divine providence."

(Martin 1983b: 101, 106)

The dream of acting with authority is complex and faces a number of pitfalls in any society. To act requires will; nothing can be done, then, without some unification of motive and intention. To act also requires that others understand how one's own purpose affects their interests; nothing can therefore be done in concert that lacks meaning. Just as a sign must be given that indicates an individual's purpose, so a symbol is required that provides insight into the relation of one purpose to another; in short, meaning. As action moves beyond the sphere of those that are immediately involved, that meaning will undergo translation from one context to another; its "publication" allows it to have significance, although that significance cannot be taken for granted and depends on the willing response of others who are not a party to the initial action. To reach the point at which an individual can hope to act with authority therefore requires a strong base in social life and in culture. That basis, I have been arguing, is steadily weakened in complex societies. As motives become irrelevant to intention, actions lose authenticity. As purposes are articulated in a society that is open to an increasing number of disparate and compartmentalized voices, the point at which multiple purposes combine becomes moot; the question of meaning becomes relatively meaningless. As actions become separated into private and public discourses, actors no longer have to agree so thoroughly on the relation of one topic, speaker, or role to another, and priorities vary with the context and with the moment; the question of an action's significance therefore depends less on its publication, so to speak, than on publicity. Under these conditions, actions seldom arrive at the fourth threshold, and when they do, their passage across that threshold is seldom aided by religious belief or ritual.

Beyond these impediments there is another barrier at the fourth threshold: a problem in the logic of social action. To act in a way that has lasting consequences in any society is to pre-empt further action. It is essential for acts to be irreversible if an actor's will is to be done; social action always implies more or less binding obligations on all those who are directly or indirectly a party to the act; otherwise there would be no law. On the other hand, of course, no action can be fulfilled in this way without stifling further action; to act on the level of an entire social system is therefore self-limiting and could become self-defeating if that system itself does not embody a principle that allows for continuing revision; such revision, however, undermines the guarantees of every enactment. Even the Constitution of the United States can therefore be amended to abrogate the Constitution itself; to do so would be entirely constitutional. The contradiction inherent in any social action is apparent at earlier thresholds; action may not fully embody the will of the actor if it is to have meaning, and its meaning may be altered as it gains significance. The contradiction becomes fully apparent, however, only at the fourth threshold, where action to be fulfilled must suspend the conditions on which it has hitherto depended.

The impediments to social action at this point, where the logic of the individual meets the logic of the social system, have attracted perhaps the lion's share of sociological interest since the outset of the discipline. Certainly the theory of alienation links the themes of self-estrangement with social action; for all its embroidery, that theory does point to an indissoluble contradiction in social life that finds eventual expression in culture generally and most particularly in religion. Durkheim has pointed to the contradiction in any system that legitimates its own authority on the welfare of the individual; this contradiction is also explored in connection with capitalism by Bell (1976: 196). Weber finds the contradiction equally indissoluble and warns against any attempt in politics or religion to act as if that contradiction could be transcended. Given the proclivity of sociologists to separate into perspectives that I have called the realist and the pragmatist, it would not be surprising to find a similar division of opinion on this topic; it is a division I wish briefly to explore, since it enables us to describe more precisely the impediments facing all action as it seeks to cross the fourth threshold.

The realist position is quite straightforward. Action seeks to complete and express itself in terms that are not only meaningful and significant but binding on others at the level of an entire system; otherwise its consequences are temporary and its significance limited therefore to actions that have no impact on a society as a whole. To be enacted, however, requires the ultimate sacrifice of the individual as an autonomous, will-ful being. The contradiction is expressed in the Christian religion, of course, in the person and work of Jesus Christ. In his work, he accomplishes *once and for all* an act that has universal and everlasting effect; it reconstitutes the authority on which every society is based. In his person, however, Jesus performs the ultimate act of self-sacrifice by wholly subordinating his will to the divine order and his well-being to the trust of others. Any departure from the full expression of this contradiction between individual authority and self-sacrifice limits the truth of the religious expression. Any society, furthermore, whose self-understanding does not approximate this full awareness of paradox and contradiction in its own life is to that extent departing from the truth. Certainly the realist position in sociology, at least *chez* Durkheim, is an attempt to explicate this contradiction.

Among contemporary sociologists David Martin has perhaps given the most consistent and extended statement of sociological realism; he speaks, for instance, of the paradox I have described as being derived from the "dualism" of Christianity itself (Martin 1978a). The paradox is grounded, so to speak, on the rock of religious truth. Martin speaks, on the one hand, of the way Christianity opposes every form of political and cultural center. The earthly king confronts a rival who carries the sword of a heavenly kingdom; the natural family faces competition from a family that is based on commitment and choice rather than on genes or on the authority of the ancestors. On the other hand, unlike the more utopian of contemporary radicals, Christianity only bites rather than destroys the hand that feeds it; there is in that faith a provisional guarantee that the family and the state will enjoy at least an edict of toleration: a favor that the state has eventually been obliged to return. Every form of dissent in Christianity therefore pays respect to the principle of order even while snubbing particular orders and setting up its own; every form of commitment in Christianity also carries within itself the slow-burning fuse of choice.

To put it another way, if Western societies have sought to institutionalize voluntarism, therefore, it is because of Christianity, even when it was despite the Church. Regardless of whether Western societies have different ways of framing political and social reality, the underlying dualism reflects a certain truth. Martin allows for the fact that one society (e.g. France) sharply limits the sphere of the Churches' operations, and bases political authority on a militant secularism, while another society (e.g. the United States) allows politics and religion freely to influence one another while the Churches and the state enjoy a formal separation; the underlying principle of the two societies nonetheless derives from the peculiar dialectic or dualism of Christianity, and to that extent these societies are exhibiting a truth that is universal if not absolute.

That is why every political or cultural center has a periphery, in Martin's scheme of things. The rationality that is the dominant principle of order enjoys opposition: from the élite, who argue that every rational order must make concessions to fairness and dignity; from a middle class, who indicate that they are as disciplined as they are self-determining and therefore uphold the principle of order even when protesting armaments or standing in silent vigil outside the university president's office; and from the least rational, perhaps, who sing their protest but, in their singing, at least follow the principles of harmony (see Martin 1978b: 60–61). The periphery is sometimes close to the center, in which case it is élitist and was, for instance, Calvinist; sometimes the periphery is further away (Methodist and middle class) or quite far removed from the center (lower class and Pentecostal) (see Martin 1978b: 60–1). The point in every case is the same, that Christianity supports and expresses a dialectic between social system and individual action that tends toward a precarious but persistent institutionalization of voluntarism in Western societies.

The pragmatist view is no less sanguine about the possibilities of institutionalizing voluntary action than the realist position I have attempted to illustrate in the work of David Martin; pragmatism even finds in this process a positive role for religion. That role, however, is temporary; religion works for a time, but it works almost despite itself and only by sustaining certain illusions; in the long run the system either fails, in which case religion may enjoy a renewed interest as individuals seek theodicies and rituals to justify and ward off such failure; or the system succeeds, and the role of religion, which is prototypically individualistic and magical in its thinking and impulse, inevitably declines to the level of action that is largely personal, arbitrary, and of no lasting significance to the system as a whole. It is convenient to typify this view of the relation of individual action to the logic of social systems in some (not all, of course) of the work of Wilson, especially since he has focused no less on "less developed" societies than on the large-scale and highly complex systems I have been concerned with in this book. In both contexts, however, Wilson's argument is the same: as individuals succeed in making their wishes effective in a social system that begins to be stable and effective, religion declines in significance; they achieve "a more rational order, as men themselves begin to take on the powers once ascribed to the gods" (Wilson [1956], 1975: 494).

The pragmatist viewpoint therefore is optimistic about action *up to a point*; the precise location of that point, of course, varies with the society in question. Where whole societies are concerned, personal reality in action is particularly subject to the demands of systemic rationality, whether that latter principle of order is embodied in sacred or secular institutions. Wilson is quite ready to accept the notion that religion preserves "the spirit of separate, authentic, cultural integrity," but not "the actuality" of such integrity ([1956], 1975: 496). Take, for example, the notion of a new Israel; the Church claimed to embody the true identity of the old Israel even though that nation had been defeated, dispersed, and overwhelmed by the forces of the Roman Empire. Granted that Christianity claims that even the tradition of such ancestors as Abraham and Moses is fulfilled in the new era, the illusion of continuity is precisely that, Wilson would argue. Contrast that reading of the role of religion at the level of a whole social system with Martin's, who would argue that only such a dualism that transcends the natural order of tribal and political descent reflects the underlying truth of any society that has come under the aegis of the Judeo-Christian tradition. Apply this difference of opinion to arguments about whether the religious nationalism of England or America represents a real or illusory integrity and identity; you will quickly see that sociological opinion will be sometimes bitterly divided over what constitutes the "truth" or the pathology of these large-scale social systems.

If the dream of authoritative action that constitutes an entire society is only an illusion in the case of tribal communities and states, how can it be any less illusory in the case of complex and pluralistic nation-states? Unlike the pragmatist, however, the sociological real-ist distinguishes between a social reality, in which claims to religious identity and integrity may indeed be illusory, and a truth which, however penultimate it may be, still applies to nations as much as to tribes; namely, that there is a fundamental contradiction between a principle of order based on the continuities of family, generation, and state and a principle of order based on the individual's will, responsibility, and capacity for effective choice. That contradiction, furthermore, finds perhaps its fullest expression in the Judeo-Christian tradition; it is that tradition, in any case, that is authoritative for Western societies. From the pragmatist viewpoint there is no mystery about this contradiction between principles of order. Any attempt to institutionalize voluntarism as the principle of order will inevitably disappoint the more grandiose aspects of the dream of the completed and irreversible act. Such an act belongs to the realm of magic, in any case; only the "thaumaturgist" can work such wonders, and Wilson describes in vivid cross-cultural detail the failure of the thaumaturgist to govern the community or society as a whole (Wilson 1956).

The differences between the two sociological viewpoints are most apparent here; that is, concerning the possibility of keeping religious ideals alive in a society that also seeks to make voluntarism a way of life. Wilson notes many cases of tribal or colonial societies that imitate the discipline of Western societies (Wilson 1956). The native leaders drill their followers, march them to the fields, train them in chants, and require them to respond with appropriate slogans: all in the name of creating a modernized social order based on the commitment and will of the individual citizen. It is beyond the natives' ken, Wilson notes, fully to appreciate how complex are the roles in a modern bureaucracy, and beyond their immediate capacity as individuals to develop the self-discipline necessary for sustaining such an order. There is no magic that can work the wonders of a rationalized social system, no matter how ritualized are the procedures adopted by those who, admitting Western power, seek Western ways.

Martin, on the other hand, notes that what appears to be passivity or helplessness or what passes for playful or useless activity carries within itself its own principle of order: its own understanding of rhythm, sequence, possibility, and of higher vision (Martin 1978b). In what the world takes to be of no account, the sociological realist finds signs of principled activity. It is precisely the vision of a sociologist, part of whose training is in the English tradition of dissent, a tradition that found in song and prayer, in quiet discipline and the long development of character the basis of a social order that could renew the life of an aging, even moribund system. If England is green, it is at least partly because it has been watered by very deep spiritual springs that only appear to be spontaneous and arbitrary when erupting on the surface; according to Martin, they flow from deep channels and underlie the center of a social system even if they only flow freely on the surface or periphery. Simply because any particular dissent may be arbitrary, willful, and short-lived is insufficient reason for the sociologist to forfeit the dream of a social system that taps and embodies the most profound individual aspirations for authentic, meaningful, significant, and enduring acts.

Like English Dissent, religious movements in many colonies that had been profoundly influenced by Western religious and political institutions did succeed in gaining some power for the natives and achieved, in many cases, some stability. The requirements of mobilizing effort over a longer period of time than is required for the thaumaturgist's usual endeavors led such movements to become more rational in providing rewards and setting limits, and such movements in order to succeed had to acquire expertise in coordinating activities and setting goals. As voluntarism becomes institutionalized, acts become not only more effective but more limited. In the long run, rationality displaces the grandiose dreams for action that is valid and effective once and for all. That is why, for instance, the watchword of announcements from the President's press secretary is so often "at this time." The President has no plans "at this time" to invade Nicaragua or to consider limiting defense expenditures or increasing taxes. Secular societies are "secular" precisely because they make commitments and adopt policies only for the time being; the requirements of adapting to changing domestic and foreign situations prohibit more enduring and complete acts than the merely strategic. While Wilson would find such action understandable and adaptive, however trivial and disappointing in its moral and intellectual dimensions, it does represent a form of civic order that the pragmatist can both predict and accept. To Martin, of course, even such pragmatism embodies a principle, and it would appear in the case of the secular state to be a principle of "what works"; as Lasch argued, it is a principle that decides to make statements, not on the basis of what is true and verifiable, but what will be believed or what the traffic of public opinion at least will bear (Lasch 1979). Such a principle of order is not new, of course, and precisely because it is a principle of order it stands in the same place, so to speak, as any religious principle of social order. Caesar and the Temple jostle one another on the same ground. They are principles of order not merely in a "functional" sense but in the sense implied by the New Testament when it speaks of principalities and powers: the unseen but pervasive forces that order social life and provide an effective, however invisible, framework that shapes and limits even the best of intentions and most enduring of wills. What appears to the pragmatist as a rational, albeit merely strategic or formal, principle of order, is to the sociological realist evidence of a higher, however limited or distorted, principle of order. In this way the latter tradition keeps open the question of truth that is sometimes begged by sociological inquiries into the different "realities" framed by one social system or another.

Institutionalizing Voluntarism: Toward a Secular Society

There are two sociological explanations, therefore, as to why a society can institutionalize voluntarism. One emphasizes the overriding necessity of a system to get itself going and to keep going, a necessity that enforces a type of logic that is rational no matter how often appeal is made to higher, even divine authority. Work must be done and resources gathered; decisions must be made and supporters galvanized into continuous and effective action; changes must be made and decisions rescinded – all in the name of continuity, perhaps, but in the service of change. No religious dream of an act accomplished once and for all, binding on a society and significant to succeeding generations, both meaningful to believers and authentic in its original inspiration, can adequately frame the actions that are necessary not merely to initiate but to sustain a social system. On the other hand, the sociological realist would argue, no order is more vulnerable to subversion than one based on principled decision. Such an order sustains even kingship with the metaphor of a divine king, in whose name no merely earthly kingship can rule without fear of contradiction (see Martin 1978b: 1 ff.). That contradiction is inherent in the mythology of a divine kingdom: a source of metaphors that creates a dualism within any public rhetoric. On the basis of that dualism any claim to authority can be countered with a higher claim. Every decision, moreover, even one binding on the body politic, is exposed to the same contradiction; one can speak against any decision in the name of the principle of voluntarism itself, according to which no choice should undermine the basis of further choice. No constitution should be adopted that cannot forever be amended. On that contradiction, obviously, one major nation-state, the United States, was founded and still continues to founder.

Of course, it is almost impossible to imagine a society in which nothing is done once and for all; nothing lasts. A society in which an authoritative act does not last is without government except by force and whim. Furthermore, where no regime officially begins as another legitimately ends, there can be no orderly succession. One can imagine, however, a society without a stated age for retirement; there one's work would never be officially done. In an actual society without stated ages for maturity, one would never "come of age" or be entitled to certain rights or liable for certain unpleasant duties on the basis of age alone. A society without well-defined authority will not be able to recognize an unnatural act or an act of kindness; and even with the authority of common values, a society cannot proclaim kind actions to be acts of kindness unless it has the rites for such a proclamation. I am using the term "secular," then, to apply to a hypothetical society in which only actions are performed and not enduring acts. I doubt whether a society that does not foster a genuine sense of security and importance among its members can mobilize them effectively, make them work hard enough to create a surplus, postpone rewards from one generation to the next, get the young to pay for the diseases of the old, and relieve the minds of the grief-stricken about the deaths of those whom they mourn. Without adequate ritualization one generation will not sacrifice for the previous one or the next. Without a transcendent metaphor for the nation, its routines will seem hopeless and its sacrifices will seem cruel. Without a source of contradiction, the society as a whole will also lack a source of transcendent authority.

Where religion no longer provides a metaphor for the nation and, therefore, a source of contradiction, the state is free to reduce all acts to actions however trivial and absurd. The letter of the law operates without the infusion of the spirit. In the following words, Hegel very nicely summarized the most narrow judicial appraisal of the meaning of actions under the law when the religious metaphor has died; for the individual:

"the deed *alone* is to be affirmed as his genuine being – not his figure or shape, which would express what he 'means' to convey by his acts, or what anyone might 'conjecture' he merely could do. In the same way, on the other hand, when his performance and his inner possibility, capacity, or intention are opposed, the former *alone* is to be regarded as his true reality, even if he deceives himself on the point, and, after he has turned from his action into himself, means to be something else in his 'inner mind' than what he is in the act."

(Quoted from *The Phenomenology of Mind*, pp. 349–50, in O'Neill 1972: 158)

Clearly this theory would justify the refusal of the modern state to look at an action of military insubordination or civil disobedience as an act of conscientious objection. The state prefers to objectify actions into performances that it can define according to its own categories of acts. No wonder that to institutionalize voluntarism it is necessary to undermine the grounds of political authority.

In a liberal regime, as I have noted in an earlier work (Fenn 1982), the state may allow such dissidents as the Berrigans in the United States to expand at some length on their motives and intentions;

certainly the trial of the Catonsville Nine provided such an opportunity for the elaboration of the spirit in which the defendants burned government files. The liberal state may listen to such testimony only to determine that the spirit is irrelevant; their judicial conviction depends only on whether or not the defendants indeed performed certain actions – not on their religious convictions. In an authoritarian regime, however, the state inquires rather deeply into hidden motives and secret intentions. There the meaning of the performance depends on what the state can learn of the actor's spirit, whereas in a liberal regime the state can ignore the spirit and inquire simply into the performance itself. In those authoritarian regimes, like South Africa, where the state considers itself an extension of the Church, the metaphor of dualism between the nation and Church has not died so much as it has been reduced to a literal meaning: a virtual identity.

Where the religious community no longer is a metaphor for the nation, authorities may still turn actions into completed acts and guarantee the succession of one generation and regime to the next. Without the tension and implied judgment of the religious metaphor, however, the state through its courts can define an individual's actions in any categories that the state may please, without fear of contradiction. Actions undertaken in spiritual freedom may become defined as acts hostile to the state's own interests. The state can turn youth into adults who only serve official interests; the state can therefore guarantee the succession of generations without suffering by comparison with the religious community and the Church.

On the other hand, without *some* sense of organized transition and fulfillment social life becomes contentious and embittered. The same desire for finishing one stage of life in order to succeed to the next makes it necessary for us to know when one stage in life ends and the next begins. Americans are somewhat confused about when maturity begins and adolescence ends: when to start drinking, to fight for the country, to vote in elections, and to be liable for adult criminal penalties. Americans are still debating when retirement should begin and middle age end. Work may be like an indefinite sentence; one may never be able to do enough. No wonder it is part of the dissenting tradition to make such limits and stages a matter for conscientious, religious *decision*.

Just as it is necessary to know when the time has come to move from one stage in life to another, generations must be able to pass their gifts to one another: gifts of the spirit, special legacies, and offerings of respect. If one generation does not wish to receive what a prior generation is ready to give, the older generation may not prove willing to relinquish its power to the younger; the time for succession may never come.

The realist position in sociology, then, argues that a single principle in many societies, especially those that have developed under Judeo-Christian auspices, accounts for a perennial source of dissent as well as for whatever legitimacy and authority a social system can claim. To enshrine the principle that individuals should act with authority, in every sense of that term and at every level, runs the risk of making every decision reversible and open to question; no act, even in the name of the republic or commonwealth, can cease to be merely that: the work of the individual acting in concert with other individuals. On the other hand, the same principle that undermines every institution operates as the source of legitimate authority for the social system; Western societies are based on the tradition that sanctifies the conscientious decision of the individual, "so help me God." In the long run there is an accounting before the same deity who insists that every individual be accountable; on that principle kings and judges as well as presidents and ministers have held their several offices. It is a principle that cuts away at every loyalty to clan or tribe, locale or ethnic group, that is based on natural or other affinities rather than choice. Even the state can insist that rights be respected regardless of such natural affinities, and even the state legitimately can take these local or ethnic ties into consideration in allocating its rewards to individuals. The ethic by which individuals take to themselves the powers once attributed to gods (i.e. to create the social world in their image) is a sacred one, whether or not it leads to an administration that is cruel or just, impersonal or alert to the distinct and incommensurate needs of the individual in whose name it claims authority.

Rituals in a Secular Society: the Attempt to Ritualize Voluntarism

In retrospect, one can see the various efforts to remodel traditional liturgies in modern societies as a further stage in the institutionalization of voluntarism, a stage in which the contradictions I have been discussing would be transcended in ritual. The system itself would require what individuals seek: an arena for choice in the acts that constitute the system itself. Through ritual, the system would seek to neutralize sources of contradiction in various ways: by limiting as well as providing for discretion by the laity; by providing a speech which combines the public with the private so as to ensure a single discourse and to eliminate private sources of dissent; and by requiring that change itself occur in areas, including the rites themselves, that many individuals might seek to leave intact. I have already discussed the ways in which modern rites provide for and yet limit options, locate differing and potentially conflicting wishes in discrete liturgical contexts, and provide a veneer of ordinary speech in the new rites that appears to transcend the gap between public and private discourse. Here I will focus on the introduction of new rites as being in itself an exercise in institutionalizing and therefore limiting voluntarism in the life of one modern society. The illustrations, as before, come primarily from the English case, where the rites of the Anglican Church still embody acts that are defined as belonging to the society as a whole, the Church being established, as it were, regardless of the rates of public attendance and private unbelief. The acts by which the *Book of Common Prayer* were revised were authorized by acts of the English Parliament and could not otherwise have occurred. There was serious dissent, however, over whether the Church's rites should be revised; take, for example, the debate in the House of Commons, on 4 December, 1974, over the "Worship and Doctrine Measure," a bill that would permit the Church of England to authorize forms for worship that would be alternatives to the *Book of Common Prayer* – an increase of discretion for the Church that would provide more autonomy although not outright independence. Parliament would retain the role of final arbiter of disputes over the Church's worship. In that debate, two members spoke as follows:

"Parliament, with the Queen, is sovereign over the Church. Let us therefore say to the professionals and to those who want to take over our Church: 'We are the people. It is our Church, You shall not have it.'" (Ivor Stanbrook, MP)

"I shall not vote for it. I am not sure whether I shall vote against it ... the General Synod and the general organization ... are out of touch with the man in the pew. I regard myself as the typical man in the pew." (Andrew Bowden, MP; he did vote against it) (Quoted in *News of Liturgy*, Issue 3, March 1975: 2).

Now, in the light of these impassioned and forthright statements by two Members of Parliament on behalf of the laity, the following editorial comment by Colin Buchanan is ample evidence of the degree to which Mr Bowden was right that "the general organization [is] out of touch with the man in the pew":

> "The whole seven hours leaves one amazed at the zeal of members, equally amazed at the ignorance of many (both for and against), and even more amazed at the half-submerged Church of England when it actually stands up and describes the Church and its worship in this way. I have long felt on theoretical and doctrinal grounds that it was wrong, in a post-Christendom situation, that Parliament should have final control over worship. But I now find the sheer a posteriori *pragmatic* argument even stronger. The vaunted attempt to speak for 36 million people left each one speaking only for himself."
>
> (*News of Liturgy*, Issue 3, March 1975: 2)

Adding to Mr Buchanan's amazement, I should add, was the fact that the measure, although it passed, drew forty-five negative votes in the Commons, whereas a prior measure enabling the Church to undertake liturgical revision, had received no negative votes whatsoever.

Mr Buchanan, a member of the Church of England's Liturgical Commission, was convinced that the Members of Parliament who spoke against the new forms of worship spoke for themselves alone. This conviction did not prevent him from airing a similarly negative opinion in the pages of his newsletter, from which the following excerpt will give the flavor:

Professor C. R. Dunstan:

> "The Church of England to-day professes Incarnation – but practices withdrawal: it is tearing up its roots from the land, the life, the culture, the social sinews and institutions. ... At a time when our whole society calls aloud for the spiritual regeneration of which the Church ought to be the agent, the Church dissipates its resources in an adolescent preoccupation with its own identity."
>
> (*News of Liturgy*, Issue 9, September 1975: 1)

In the same issue, he published a rejoinder from a priest who protested against being led by Professor Dunstan back into "pluralism, patronage, Prince Bishops, Parliamentary control and pigs in the parsonage" (p. 2).

In the first four Christian centuries ritual was intended to provide a password, a critical test of an individual's faith and commitment, but the new rituals have been themselves the object of testing in the light of the individual's own religious orientation. Whether the individual is a liturgical scholar or a lay person saddened by the loss of words and phrases once learned by heart is for the moment irrelevant. It is ritual that now stands to be tested by individual conviction. In this new relationship of ritual to social life, rituals have been called "trial liturgies," since they are indeed on trial for their very life. Liturgies have never been entirely autonomous and self-justifying, of course. Especially in the Reformed tradition, the liturgy is tried in the light of Scripture and before the bar of lay opinion, for worship without scriptural authority is unwarranted (see Sykes 1978: 91), but when rituals are themselves on trial, they do not stand in a position to bring the loyalties and grievances of the world before the throne of ultimate judgment.

Ours, or course, is not the first period of skepticism and of constant testing of old and new rituals, and with fresh inspiration in such a period individuals will freely undertake a wide range of new roles. During the Reformation the Protestant faith enabled individuals to pursue their salvation with whatever fear and trembling, outside the cloisters and without benefit of clergy. The Reformation not only made traditional authority precarious or unnecessary, it enabled individuals to undertake unprecedented economic or political risks and therefore to develop new roles in government and industry. The full supply of such a faith, once it spread among marginal groups and became institutionalized in the larger society, made it possible for the Church and state, each with a vested interest in controlling individuals, to ask fewer questions and grant a wider range of social and religious liberties. New knowledge was therefore generated not only in the twilight of traditional authority but in the dawn of new theories – of new visions of the order of things. Science prospered along with industry and democratic institutions. The increase of religious faith made possible new undertakings in work and politics, while these new undertakings seek authority in revisions of religious orthodoxy. The dialectic between faith and authority, once restored, found liturgical expression.

I question whether individual freedom and social authority will now be able to find common liturgical ground. *The new rituals are local options, and the nation as a whole is never called to repentance and seldom to thanksgiving.* There is a dearth of ritual at the level of the nation at a time when some groups still apparently wish that both England and America could rid themselves of certain impure elements in the body politic, perhaps through a final and violent confrontation. The self-esteem of certain groups is still threatened by the pride and grievances of others who resent being displaced from their ancestral lands onto reservations, or who have come only lately to British or American soil. Vengeance only belongs to the Lord above when through ritual the past can be completed and finished, done with and undone, transfigured once and for all. Where rituals themselves are "on trial," social life may for the time being preserve only a fragile civility. That civility is fragile indeed.

There is nothing particularly new in this criticism of the pragmatic quality of the new rites and of the pragmatism which justified their introduction to the laity. On the contrary, the field of sociology has been marked from the outset by lengthy diatribes against pragmatism; another such polemic is unnecessary here. It might be helpful, however, to mention briefly some of Durkheim's objections to pragmatism; they are very much like my own caveats against the revision of the old rites and the content of the new ones. As Durkheim put it in his lectures on pragmatism immediately prior to the First World War, pragmatism is born of a desire to "soften" the truth:

"to take from it this absolute and as it were sacrosanct character. It is to tear it away from this state of immobility that removes it from all becoming, from all change and, consequently, from all explanation."

(Durkheim [1955], 1982: 65)

Durkheim knew, as well as any pragmatist, that reality is socially constructed. Therefore reality is mutable and malleable, relative to one social context, and yet pluralistic because reality has many such contexts. Because it is social, reality is also profoundly personal and subjective; it inheres in the mind of the individual. Reality, however, is not to be confused with the truth, and as Durkheim reminded his students, there is always something external, impersonal, and imposing or constraining about the truth:

"men have always recognized in truth something that in certain respects imposes itself on us, something that is independent of the facts of sensitivity and individual impulse."

(Durkheim [1955], 1982: 68)

Unfortunately, if Durkheim is correct (see p. 54), the pragmatism, at least of William James, was not very effective in separating the question of how reality is constructed from the question of truth.

It may not be entirely fair to the liturgical revisors to argue that they begged the truth question. In the United States, as I shall later point out, at least one liturgist (Holmes 1981) associated with changing the *Book of Common Prayer* notes that the purpose of the revision was to change doctrine. In making this statement he concedes to those who opposed the revision the major point that more was at stake than the forms of worship: the content of Christian teaching was indeed the issue. The new rites were intended to serve as educational devices to upgrade and update the Church's teaching. It would be difficult, however, to find a more pragmatist viewpoint on the function of liturgy than to assert that it is an instrument for teaching; Dewey would have entirely understood.

There are other aspects of pragmatism that are readily apparent in the fact and mode of liturgical change. The rites were "trial" liturgies; the approach was as experimental, in certain respects, as Dewey's notion of inquiry. One experimental rite succeeded another, until more of the laity found them suitable, convenient, or satisfying. It was precisely these pragmatist criteria (e.g. of various forms of utility) that Durkheim found lacking as ways of assessing the truth. If, as Durkheim noted of the English pragmatist, Schiller, "man is the measure of all things" (Durkheim [1955], 1982: 55) there can be no doubt that pragmatism is right to assess any social practice in terms of its convenience or ability to satisfy most people most of the time. It is "right," if one is assessing not the truth but reality. Certainly individuals do cooperate in the making of reality; and in this cooperation their experience is no doubt central. Durkheim has no difficulty in accepting such a viewpoint from Schiller, since it is one to which sociology itself adheres very closely. The problem that concerned Durkheim, however, was the question of truth. If humans are indeed the measure of humankind, who takes the measure of humans?

Pragmatism is sociological in part, but it is not sufficiently sociological to face the truth question. No doubt that one measure of the new rites is indeed the way in which they were received and experienced by various groups of individuals; that is precisely the point. The satisfaction or convenience of these groups arises not from mere experience unadorned with social categories and constraints; on the contrary, these groups measured their experience in terms of categories that existed, so to speak, prior to their experience. There is no way that the new rites could be assessed apart from the contexts in which they were tried, and the assessments inevitably reflected those contexts. The liturgical committees in fact preferred the criteria of some social groups and their contexts over others: the "new estates" in England were given preference over the experience and criteria of, say, the elderly, the rural, and the relatively uneducated members of the English population. The trials were based, then, on received notions and categories; the results reflected both the views of the experimenters and the nature of the social laboratories in which the experiments were conducted. Inquiry and experimentation were artifacts of the pre-existing social worlds in which the Church chose to operate. If reality is to be shaped, it will be shaped, as Durkheim might have put it, according to the contours of the social context. That context is indeed the subject of this book, and it extends beyond the suburbs and "new estates" to committees and office buildings, to the enclaves of scholarship and to the higher reaches of ecclesiastical administration. In tracing the efforts of the Churches to shape Christian reality, therefore, we will be monitoring the efforts of certain pragmatists to "soften the truth" and to make it less "sacrosanct."

Dualism Explored Further

What indeed is this "truth" for our time? Certainly the new liturgy places all nations in a relativistic limbo approaching, but falling short of, the purposes and glory of God. The reformers have little liturgical use for a piety directed toward the nation. The laity are required to fix their hopes not on the nation but on the emergence of an international order of Christian people whose unity is itself a sign of the historical progress of the Kingdom of God. The people's prayers for secular authority will therefore vary little whether they are uttered in Islamic or secular states or ones, like the United Kingdom, where some of the people still dare to hope, if no longer to pray, for a Christian nation. Instead of a dualism between civic order and the order of choice, there appears to be not much to choose among nations.

The new rituals have removed the label of "Christian" from the mention of earthly rulers and place Queen Elizabeth or the President of the United States in the same twilight of authority as the Ayatollah and the Politburo. Once adopted by the Church, such a ritual disestablishes political authority without the passage of a single statute or constitutional amendment. The nation no longer serves God through the state in any sense peculiar to that nation's own faith, but the state serves instead only in the name of certain abstract values such as harmony and justice – values that receive the same devotion from Marxists and Muslims as they do from Christians and Jews. A ritual that prescribes international texts for the recital of an increasing number of prayers limits the authority of the laity's own social and emotional ties to their communities and ethnic groups, to their nation and to their friends. The ties are dissolved in a textual acid that eats away all but the most universal and international forms of community life.

The liturgical reformers may have wished to kill the dream of a Christian nation, because the national establishment of religion had prevented the adoption of a new book in 1928. Indeed, Gladstone predicted in the last century that if the Church were to undergo more liturgical controversies at the parliamentary level, the establishment itself would not endure, as the Church would feel compelled to seek the purity of its mission in international terms beyond the scope and confines of the nation. But similar imperatives did not constrain the other Anglican Churches that also have moved quickly to adopt international texts, stoic prayers for harmony and justice, and toward a reduction of the sacramental role of the laity to religious consumers or to emissaries sent on the errands of the Church in a secular world. What is needed, I argue in the concluding chapter, is a theological recovery of the full dimensions of the metaphor relating Church to nation.

In the next chapter I turn briefly to some speeches by Cromwell to suggest one form that Christian dualism may take in Western societies. Some will find Cromwell a poor choice; certainly he suppressed the *Book of Common Prayer* as a royalist document, although Firth reminds us that Cromwell tolerated the continued worship of Anglican congregations and argued for the continued public support of the clergy through a system of tithes (Firth 1966: 346 ff.). Americans may find Cromwell a more sympathetic figure, of course, than would the English; Americans have seen their nation united by force under a President who gave serious theological and pious thought to the use of the sword. Cromwell, of course, was more concerned with tolerating those, whether of Anglican or Independent persuasion, who were not actively or in principle committed to the overthrow of the government by force – a principle of exclusion that Americans understand only too well. What makes Cromwell so intriguing a guide, however, is not just a passing resemblance to Abraham Lincoln or his command of the preaching that led colonists to see themselves as a city upon a hill. Granted that what some sociologists now see as an American "civil religion" finds ample expression in the texts of Cromwell's speeches to Parliament, I find in those speeches something more useful: a frank use of the metaphor of the people of God as a means of defining the nature of the nation under the aspect of God's providential purpose in history. The tension between Church and nation that permeates that metaphor can only too easily be lost when either the Church or the nation attempts to cut its ties to the other. A full understanding of that metaphor in England's political theology makes that tension come alive, with good effect, I would argue, both for the Church and for the nation in their relation to the state.

Whether the Church can be an effective metaphor for the nation-state depends on issues that were raised but have not been settled either by the English or the American civil wars. The American states are now within a very short distance, in fact, of calling for a constitutional convention that might well stipulate the use of Christian prayer in the schools and even define the nation itself in Christian terms. Of course, a providential ordering of a nation's affairs cannot be won either in Parliament or in a constitutional convention, but Cromwell may have been more certain of that than are current advocates of reform in this country. In the Civil War the battle over the relation of the people of God to the nation-state was articulated, if not resolved, on each level of English society. There is room, here, for pragmatist thinking, but I prefer the realist position that I have described earlier. In the relation of private morality to civic virtues, in the selection of the clergy, in the honor due to members of various classes, and in such economic decisions as how to lend at interest, there were no doubt a large number of strategic considerations cloaked in religious ideas; for example, Cromwell's need for allies, for capital, and for domestic support (see Firth 1966). I am simply arguing that in the seventeenth century one can observe more clearly some of the battles that must be fought between collective and personal proprieties. In the emergence of a strong, however tense, relation between the people of God and the nation-state, short-term considerations (e.g. the requirements of a Christian nation for peace from its neighbors) vie with long-term aspirations; hence doctrines of providence must balance notions of a final judgment in history against the evidence for special divine favors and exemptions in the present. It is politically significant whether the hand of God is expected to be imminent and immanent or open and above board only at the distant end of history. The difference spells out the degrees of freedom that can be tolerated between a Christian people and the nation-state. The fewer those degrees, the more rigidly defined is the relation of the Church to the nation.

What is at stake here is the tension (Martin's dualism) between a public order based on various civic, political, moral, or natural affinities and the principle of choice itself: of order versus a will informed by Christian faith and doctrine. In discussing Abraham Lincoln's theological reflections on the Civil War, Niebuhr gives that President very high praise. Lincoln's:

> "combination of moral resoluteness about the immediate issues with a religious awareness of another dimension of meaning and judgement must be regarded as almost a perfect model of the difficult but not impossible task of remaining loyal and responsible toward the moral treasures of a free civilization on the one hand while yet having some religious vantage point over the struggle."
>
> (Niebuhr 1952: 172)

In the light of these "treasures" or social "realities," Lincoln made moral judgments and used force; he was not loath to see the hand of a special providence in history working out its purposes through the American Civil War. But Lincoln also found himself unwilling to judge his adversaries and felt obligated to rule out malice in favor of charity "toward all"; he also found theological support for condemning slavery. His sense of the limits set by God on any order prevented Lincoln from claiming divine judgment on the controversy between North and South in the Civil War; his respect for the orders of his society, however, allowed him to believe that God's "purposes could not annul the moral purposes of men who were 'firm in the right as God gives us to see the light'" (Niebuhr 1952: 171–72). Like Cromwell and even like Governor Winthrop, Lincoln knew of a city whose shining would illumine other nations if its light were allowed to burn brightly enough in American institutions; he also knew that the shining of that light depended for its brilliance on "an overarching providence whose purposes partly contradicted and were yet not irrelevant to the moral issues of the conflict" (p. 171). The nation cannot complete itself without suspending judgment; on the other hand, the Christian faith cannot complete itself without taking root in a soil where it mixes with other ingredients such as local loyalties and mistaken judgments. Ambiguity and tension did not immobilize Lincoln, however, any more than the problematic metaphor immobilized Cromwell. On the contrary, it was the tension in the metaphor that required them to act without seeking the last word or permitting others to pre-empt a final judgment on the conflict.

"Mercies" was a key term for Cromwell, and it is central to Niebuhr's own theology of God's work in history. It may be useful, therefore, to note how Niebuhr speaks of the merciful acts of God. Of course, Niebuhr uses the term conventionally, as when he speaks of Lincoln's "sense of gratitude for the divine mercies which are promised to those who humble themselves" (p. 174). Niebuhr also, however, speaks of "grace": "the virtue which arises not from pure disinterestedness but from the provisional coincidence between the interests of a ruling group within a nation and the interests of a powerful imperial community and the wider community of nations its power helps to organize" (Niebuhr 1951: 222). By some happy coincidence between its own interests in survival, for instance, and the need of the larger society, some forms of monarchy and aristocracy have survived in countries that were not directly exposed to revolutionary class struggle. Britain, for instance, maintains a more flexible relation between center and periphery than those societies, like Soviet Russia and France, that witnessed the defeat of the declining classes and their protective institutions such as the monarchy (Niebuhr 1951: 227). There has been a provisional and providential coincidence between the expansion of "modern bourgeois society" and the nations who have been both helped and exploited by their contact with the West (p. 223). The point is simply that the indeterminate, self-interested, and often corrupt or unjust assertions of rising classes, such as the bourgeoisie, have not been without redeeming features; a larger good has been served that was beyond the capacity or intention of the initial parties to ensure. In the relation of the United States to the countries of America, both North and South, whatever preliminary good has been achieved through competitive development and trade has not, perhaps, been obscured by the interests of the United States in maintaining or extending its control. Ancient good, although not fully intended by a militant American class of traders and industrialists, has become increasingly uncouth the more it has failed to benefit those who have been required to cooperate and to produce. The unmerited grace of God in history, Niebuhr might have added, can be withdrawn, as the nations are left only to increasingly bitter and self-righteous conflicts with one another.

In the populist theology of Cromwell, as in Lincoln's own theological reflections on the role of warfare and suffering in the providential shaping of a people's history, there is some role for penitence and thanksgiving; as Niebuhr put it, some "awe before the vastness of the historical drama" and some "contrition" over one's own failings. In current vainglorious American judgments on the communist nations as godless or evil, one finds little dependence on providence and even less occasion to hope for self-restraint, reconciliation, and a future in which former enemies contribute to a common good. The purely populist elements in the Protestant faith have combined with nationalist pretensions in a rhetoric that mutilates the theological perspective that Christian statesmen, even warriors like Cromwell, have brought to the use of force in building nations. The current use of providence as a whip with which to chastise America's enemies contrasts nicely with the position taken by the Archbishop of Canterbury after England's victory in the Falkland Islands; he appealed for reconciliation, while others were engaged in a purely secular jubilation over Britain's triumph. To this observer, that appeal is not inconsistent with Cromwell's sense of a providence that includes divine judgment even on the favored nations.

Niebuhr warns about the provocations of overweening national power. Consider Niebuhr's rather dim view of the spiritual achievements of any nation; collectively, humans have little capacity for the long view and tend to need short-term successes to ward off despair. Some, however, like West, see in a providential framework a reasonable calling to a nation to sacrifice and hope, even when the nation-state's very existence is put at risk:

"government lives under the Cross. No political institution has the right to eternal life. Its security is never the ultimate value. There are times when the state must learn to renounce power without foreseeing all the consequences of such renunciation, and above all without having the resources to counter them. . . . There are times when even government must accept the Cross, lose its function, and trust in God's power to raise the dead."

(West 1978: 14–15)

This position moves beyond functionalism, Cromwell, Niebuhr, and the various formulations of proponents or interpreters of putative civil religions. Here West closes the gap between the pacifist alternative in Christian thought and pragmatic Christian reflection on the give-and-take of politics within the framework of national sovereignties. *To institutionalize voluntarism at the level of the nation-state means to hold open the possibility of national self-sacrifice.*

Whether nation-states can be held to the requirements of the faith is the subject of my concluding chapter. It is not clear whether a nation has ever been able to renew itself at the same springs that give spiritual renewal to individuals. It remains doubtful whether nations can reach the same spiritual heights (or depths) as can an individual who vacillates between the extremes of hope and despair, self-seeking and self-sacrifice. Nonetheless, even Niebuhr, who normally drew a sharp line to distinguish collective from personal virtues, thought nations might perish for the same reasons as individuals: through prideful and arrogant disregard of their own limits and the rights of others. It was easier for Niebuhr to imagine that nations perish from the same sins as do individuals than to believe that, like individuals, nations may repent and be saved from their sins. I am arguing, however, that nothing short of national repentance, even to the point of national self-sacrifice, may be required of a faithful nation.

7

The Death of the Dream?

At the beginning of this book I argued that the religious dream of action that is completed once and for all is profoundly social; it cannot be fulfilled, therefore, on any level short of the largest social context in which action is taken. That context, in modern societies, is the nation-state. There can be little doubt, from the argument in these chapters, that I have no confidence that the religious dream can be acted out in societies so complex and specialized as the modern nation. At each threshold of action, I have argued, there are far too many impediments, so that the Churches are unable to provide a rite of passage. At the first threshold there are too many options and too little constraint to require the individual to expunge and purify the unconscious of motives that do not befit the intention to take an adult's role in the society. At the second threshold there are likewise so many options and separate social contexts that no single purpose is likely to be framed with others in a symbol that provides rich and overarching meaning to them all. There are too many voices and too few texts that can unify them. The third threshold is barred by other impediments; it is a virtually impassable gulf between private and public discourse. That separation of the one discourse from the other makes it impossible for individuals to agree on a discourse that would relate will and meaning to areas of public significance. It is not clear, then, whether it is the rationality of the person or of the system that matters in any specific context or what roles (i.e. the public or the private) should have priority at any given occasion.

Under these conditions, I argue, it is exceedingly difficult for action to carry out the intention of the religious dream; and at the level of the nation-state it is impossible short of national self-sacrifice. One can either jettison the dream or revise one's assessment of the nation-state as a theater of human will and action. In this chapter I suggest that the Churches are jettisoning the dream in subtle ways: by making it more literal, more limited, and more identical with the virtues and practices of everyday life. The dream is left as a set of illusions or as a hope that entirely transcends history – a radical shift, I would argue, from the Gospels' intent. If there is a social system so complex and powerful that action cannot cross the threshold at the level of the society as a whole, it may survive through apathy, self-delusion, and where necessary, repression. There is no sociological reality to which I can refer that makes it impossible for the modern nation-state to survive; even the religious dream itself can be trans-lated into terms that deprive it of revolutionary import. A society that cannot synthesize personal and systemic forms of rationality and unite public with private discourse in ritual will reduce action to other dimensions; it is still possible for a religious community to provide local meaning if not public significance to their adherents' actions, and in both Britain and the United States religious groups are demandng that their meanings be granted public significance through legislative action on abortion, civil rights, and similar issues. Nonetheless neither in law nor ritual do these societies permit the religious dream to be enacted in such a way that would permit the religious impulse to carry through in irreversible acts, say, of national charity or self-sacrifice. The call to a nation to self-sacrifice, noted at the close of the previous chapter, is hardly one that could lead either of these nations to acts of contrition and, perhaps, of genuine sacri-fice. There are nations, and not only Iran, in which that religious dream can indeed, and perhaps will, come true at the national level as well as that of the congregation or even denominational headquarters.

The Dimensions of the Metaphor

Historically the Church has been a theological metaphor for the nation, and it is especially important therefore to understand how the Church's liturgy has come to diminish the dream of a nation that is specifically Christian in faith and hope and perhaps also in charity. The Church is indeed the "new Israel," the nation that acknowledges and reflects the sovereignty of God in history through a new relationship to God in Christ. The Church, in New Testament theology, is also the "people of God," the nation of the faithful within Israel that have always waited on the coming of the Lord, although they have not always shared in the worship, let alone the political authority, of Israel itself. Beyond these historical memories carried forward from the old to the new Israel, the New Testament speaks of a Church that is a nation in a new sense: a nation that is formed from the nations of the world that have hitherto been beyond the covenant.

Even beyond the new nation emerging from the broken pieces of communal and political life in the Eastern Mediterranean of the first century, the Church sees itself as the "first fruits" of the nation that will be gathered from the four corners of the earth in the end of history, when the waters cover the sea and the glory of the Lord breaks through the final barriers to consummate His purpose in history. Both the end of history and its inner purpose are embodied in a Church whose past, present, and future define and carry out the historically true meaning of nationhood. As the inheritor of the promise to the old Israel; as the faithful people of God in every generation; as the new nation created from the fragments of existing nations and peoples; and as the first compelling evidence that the inner purpose of history will be fulfilled at the end of history – the Church stands as a theological metaphor for nation and nationhood. Given that truth, the Church cannot comfortably adopt any social reality, including its own.

In that metaphoric relation every nation may come to see its origin and historical destiny; namely, to profess and embody the purpose of God in history. It is all the more necessary therefore to understand how the metaphor is lost in the Church's self-understanding: one that sees all nations in the same abstract terms.

The metaphoric relation of Church to nation is superbly set forth in Cromwell's fifteenth address to the Second Parliament. Take the Church as the people of God who become the true nation through the acts of God in history:

"Nay, who could have forethought, when we were plunged into the midst of our troubles, that ever the People of God would have had liberty to worship God without fear of enemies."

(Cromwell 1846: 395)

In the past the nation had not permitted the people of God the full opportunity to worship in freedom or to share in the power of the state, but now the people and the nation have come together. To speak of the nation, then, is to speak also of the people of God in a single metaphor, "the Nation" itself. Cromwell asks:

"But what's the reason, think you, that men slip in this age wherein we live? As I told you before, they understand not the works of God."

(Cromwell 1846: III, 398)

These are the works of a God who has "broken in pieces the powers that were." In words that echo the Church's worship, Cromwell exults that the prayers of the people – namely, to worship without fear of their enemies – have been answered by the mercy of God. As in the Magnificat, so in Cromwell's address, God is praised for a merciful act that reverses the distribution of power and authority in this world. Those who lacked the freedom to worship and the liberty to frame the country's laws now have tasted "that most significant and greatest 'mercy' the Nation hath felt or tasted" (1846:111, 345). Cromwell takes the language of the *Book of Common Prayer,* itself a liturgical setting of the prayers of the old as well as of the new Israel, and finds in its psalms and prophecies the metaphor for interpreting the national experience to those who have the ears of a faith. It is a revolutionary experience of will, expressed in meaningful purpose and significant action enacted at the highest level. It was also sectarian action carried out at considerable cost to the "enemies" of God.

The people of Cromwell's revolt no doubt had populist passions and leaders, and saw themselves as the people of the land who carry the purposes of God in their heart and become the people of God. The nation is an England whose spiritual and civil liberties inhere in the merciful acts of God. In understanding its own history the nation therefore carries forward the Church's mission: to witness to the purposes of God and to foreshadow their eventual triumph within history. Cromwell, because he is biblical in theology, takes history with proper seriousness. In the dream the Church carries the code to the nation's destiny, and the nation fulfills the vocation of the Church.

Like the nation of Israel, the union under Cromwell is a coming together of those who have settled the land under adverse circumstances and particularly under the threat of foreign power. The

English settlers in Ireland, Cromwell argued, have a momentary peace, with the Irish driven to the West and the popish powers temporarily at bay. In Scotland the "meaner sort" of peasantry have enough to eat for the first time in years. But the new Nation is a union beset by internal as well as foreign dangers. The army in Ireland is without pay. The army in Scotland is similarly precarious. Without the soldiery the settlers may have to give up their own footholds, and the union itself may then founder (Cromwell 1846: III, 418-19). Furthermore, the Catholic prince, the King of Hungary, has imperial designs that may threaten the new Protestant union from abroad (1846: III, 406). In the dream the new union is a nation marked by "peace and Gospel," formed from several peoples and through much suffering; it is also still precariously placed on the edges of the old empire – a clear historical parallel with the new Israel, the Church, formed through the breaking down of old barriers and the forming of a new community on the edge of the Roman Empire.

The Church of the seventeenth century still carried the dream in which the new Christian nation comes into being, and that dream represents the end toward which the nation strives. As Cromwell says:

"We have seen and heard and felt the evils of War ... and now God hath given us a new taste of the benefits of peace. Have you not had such a peace in England, Ireland, and Scotland, that there is not a man to lift up his finger to put you into distemper? Is not this a mighty blessing from the Lord of Heaven? Shall we now be prodigal of time."

(1846: III, 422)

Cromwell's commitment to the cause of civil liberty anticipates vindication before the seat of heavenly judgment, and in his speeches to Parliament and in his letters he frequently refers to his quarrel and to the mighty acts of God by which his cause has been vindicated. The sense of participation in a lawsuit with God as one's advocate, witness, and final judge is at the heart of much Old Testament theology; we are therefore able to understand the seriousness of Cromwell's speech only if we place the legal and judicial language of his many letters and speeches in the context of a divine law in which the Lord of history prosecutes His cause with His people. It is the same lawsuit, of course, that comes to completion in the trial and execution of Jesus, in which the nations of the world are judged. The suit continues to be prosecuted by the testimony of the faithful, by preaching in the Spirit and the Word of God, and by the signal events by which God gives his enemies into the hands of Cromwell:

"The Nature of this Cause, and the Quarrel, what that was at the first, you all very well know; I am persuaded most of you have been actors in it: It was the maintaining of the Liberty of the Nations; our Civic Liberties as Men, our Spiritual Liberties as Christians . . . nay, who could have forethought, when we were plunged into the midst of our troubles, That even the people of God should have had liberty to worship God without fear of enemies?"

(1846: III, 392, 395)

These words make clear that Cromwell's theology is neither a simple ideology for the revolution nor a utopia that suspends all historical judgment. The Spirit prosecutes and advocates the divine cause in history, and although specific events may testify to divine judgment, that judgment is not coerced by events. When action crosses the fourth threshold, so to speak, it becomes open to a fifth that may reverse all that has been accomplished.

In this framework it is possible to develop the historical dimensions of the metaphor one step further. I have pointed to Cromwell's use of the people of God, of the nation itself, and of the new union emerging from the several nations at the fringe of the continental empire, as based on the biblical use of the Church as a metaphor for the nation called by God to be his witness among the nations of the earth. The Church as the new Israel, which also began with an announcement of liberty to captives, food for the hungry, and an end to official abuses, is clearly here the metaphor by which Cromwell speaks of the nation that England may yet come to be through the merciful judgment of God in history.

It is the unity of these four themes that fully constitutes the religious dream of the Nation: the people of God, the actual nation, the emerging union, and the Last Judgment in which the Nation is both on trial and a divine witness. The gradual dissolution of this complex dream or image reduces the theological meaning to purely sociological terms of reference which beg the question of truth.

The Dying of the Metaphor

If Cromwell is right, the English are called to be, and therefore cannot yet fully be the people of God. Contrast the Cromwellian imagery with more recent theological commentary, in which the English have become merely godly people. Underhill speaks of their "sturdy and disciplined faithfulness," "distinctive religious attitude," and the "characteristic response of the English soul to the demand of God" (Underhill 1937: 318). Underhill leaves no room for doubt that she is speaking here in sociological terms. To make the point, I will quote her at more length:

> "we tend as a race [sic] to give works priority over faith, to equate religion with goodness, and to estimate worship by its this-worldly effects in terms of the moral will, rather than by its power of lifting up the mind and heart unto God. This spiritual temper . . . is fundamental to the national character."
>
> (Underhill 1937: 318)

The people of God who provide a foretaste of the emerging nation and so carry the work of God in history toward a certain, if not necessarily favorable, day of judgment have thus become merely a people whose spiritual qualities define the national character. This transition from theological prophecy to sociological description reduces the religious dream to a simple accomplishment of action in terms of will and meaning.

It is positive to find in the English soul such spiritual characteristics as being rather practical and down-to-earth, but Underhill avoids the negative motives and purposes that may give the lie to such positive intentions and embracing symbols: moral pride and egotism in the English themselves. That pride may be inferred from Underhill's modest reference to the English as a race typically concerned with works and goodness, especially when she goes on to mention the "grave beauty and sanctifying power" of those English souls most completely representative of these spiritual qualities (p. 318). But the note of judgment on the historical community is relatively absent. Granted that the English soul needs to be stimulated by a liturgy "emphasizing the holiness, authority, and total action of the Church," that liturgy will also be truly English only if it is sober and concerned with the "needs, problems, and duties of everyday life in a relatively unceremonious style and language" (p. 323).

The lack of a strong theological language open to negative as well as to positive meanings may account for the lack of metaphoric power in the English of the revised liturgy. The new versions of the confession have removed the phrase in which the people of God acknowledge that there is no "health" in them. The original meaning of health was so metaphoric as to include not only soundness of mind and body but also spiritual soundness and even salvation. As Brook notes in her analysis of the language of the *Book of Common Prayer*, even the phrase "thy saving health" is tautological, since the Old English roots incorporate both meanings in a single term connoting both wholeness and holiness (Brook 1965: 47). The English soul, as it survives in the old version of the *Book of Common Prayer*, was therefore less literal than the modern. While Underhill traces the this-worldly, activistic and practical character of the English back to medieval forms of devotion and worship, that same character found original expression in theological terms that joyfully anticipated both fulfillment and judgment. Because of that anticipation, the notion of the people of God implicitly completed and corrected any references to the laity as the people of a godly nation.

The tendency in contemporary Anglicanism for theological metaphors to become more literal and sociological is not limited to Underhill. In writing on the defining characteristics ("Integrity") of Anglicanism, Sykes (1978) draws similarly sociological parallels between the people of God (the Church) and the English people. Anglicanism is typically English, he argues, because it exhibits a "juridical" habit of thought and speech (Sykes 1978: 39–40, 45). The people of God are no longer a foretaste of an emerging nation so much as a representative sample of an existing nation. The English are agreed on fundamentals, he argues, and can therefore be contentious about practicalities and details: committed to a few central values and beliefs and therefore free to be pragmatic without losing hope or faith.

Sykes argues not only that the laity as the people of God are given to juridical argument because they are English, but that controversies over the liturgy itself carry forward juridical argument about such fundamental aspects of social life as power and authority in the Church. Note again the shift towards a sociological frame of reference and away from a metaphor pointing toward the Last Judgment. The task of doctrinal theology, according to Sykes, is therefore to focus on the social relationships and practices by which the Church adopts and uses the liturgy – a far cry from the rhetoric of Cromwell. I am arguing that the juridical habit (to which Sykes refers) is a secularized version of the biblical understanding of the people of

God, whose life is a continuous testing and trial, filled with causes and quarrels, carried to the throne of divine judgment and mercy. Sykes takes the juridical habit of mind as a given, a piece of the data. What is therefore given to the hand of the theologian is no longer a relationship betwen God and the people of God but sociological observations, the data from which the theologian draws inferences about the Church's own doctrine. Here, quoted at some length, is the way Sykes puts it:

> "The most satisfactory public statement of the Anglican view of authority [i.e. the 1948 Lambeth Conference Report that] sees the elements in authority as an ongoing process of describing the data, ordering them, mediating and verifying them."
>
> (Sykes 1978: 87)

On the strength of this invitation to an inductive theological process, Sykes points to two sets of data. The first are liturgical changes submitted to the laity and "ordinary" clergy by the "leadership" of the Church. These liturgical changes call for the regular reading of Scripture, in the light of which the laity may evaluate the new versions of the liturgy and so test the authority of the Church's leadership. The laity thus exercise a "conservative" role in "checking" the initiatives of Church's leadership – a role that produces conflict, thrives on ambiguity, and calls for discernment (pp. 94–6):

> "The point which I am concerned to sustain is that it is of the essence of the Anglican view of authority that it should be maintained in principle that the means of judging matters concerning the faith are in that hands of the whole people of God by reason of their access to the Scriptures; and, further, that it is distinctively Anglican that this means is given to them in the liturgy of the Church, backed by common law."
>
> (Sykes 1978: 93)

The people of God are no longer a nation engaged in litigation with the God of history through a series of historical events and political quarrels. The people are here reduced to a remnant saved for the purpose of evaluating new liturgical forms written elsewhere for their edification and consumption; not a noble role, but one to which they may be admitted. *The authority of the laity as the people of God has been reduced to a part in a process that itself constitutes religious authority.*

This typically Anglican "process" provides the data from which the Anglican theologian divines the Church's own doctrine of authority. The praxis of the Church defines and reveals what then becomes the doctrine of the Church through skilled theological observation and interpretation.

Recovering the Metaphor: A Note on Niebuhr and Gladstone

Let me now return to Underhill's definition of what is unique in the spirit of English worship: a comprehensive, ordered, sober, prophetic, biblical, but Catholic, sacramental, and theocentric worship (Underhill 1937: 323–24). Underhill speaks of a "national cultus" emerging from the Tudor Settlement rather than of a national polity that demands and fulfills a Christian framework (pp. 324–26). I find in the following words of Niebuhr a precise commentary on Underhill's confidence in the spirit to fulfill itself *regardless* of historical factors:

> "This pride of mystic otherworldliness makes the human spirit, not the master of history, but the agent of its own emancipation from history."
>
> (Niebuhr 1949a: 11, 305)

Let the national establishment of religion come and go; indeed, let the nation itself collapse as a framework for Christian obedience. If Underhill is right, the English spirit will find its proper and fulfilling liturgical form. I prefer Niebuhr for the following reason.

Niebuhr is very explicit about the assumptions underlying a Christian approach to history. That approach takes seriously the unique role of every nation and historical community. Niebuhr knows that individuals in their spiritual life transcend their national communities (and so would understand Underhill's perspective). But he knows also that individuals have an "indirect relation to eternity" in and through their historical communities; nations far outlast the life-span of the single person and contribute to the historical accomplishment of God's purpose in history (1953: 11, 308ff.). These historical communities, the nations in a biblical sense, reflect the mercy of God in their origin and variety and His judgment in their eventual collapse whether through fatal omissions or active transgressions (pp. 305-36). Individuals remember what civilizations forget; thus individual purposes cannot entirely be fulfilled in the civilizations and communities that impart these purposes to the individual. But nations must suffer judgment from the God who calls them into historical freedom out of the constraints of nature. Niebuhr adds:

> "The idea of resurrection [of the body and more generally of all individuals] is more social [than the idea of the immortality of the soul] because the historical constructions of human existence, the cultures and civilizations, the empires and nations and finally the whole historical process are, just as individual life, the product of a tension between natural conditions and the freedom which transcends nature. The idea of the resurrection implies that the historical elaborations of the richness of creation, in all their variety, will participate in the consummation of history. It gives the struggles in which men engaged to preserve civilizations, and to fulfill goodness in history, abiding significance and does not relegate them to a meaningless flux, of which there will be no echo in eternity."
>
> (Niebuhr 1949a: 11, 312)

To reduce the complexity of Niebuhr's theological position for the sake of this discussion, I will focus on two propositions. Both are theological, but they have sociological corollaries. The first states simply that the law is as important to the Gospel as the Gospel is to the law. The second states, somewhat less simply, that events in time have their significance as parts of a whole that is more truly historical for appearing at the end of history rather than before or beyond history in some timeless realm of spiritual purity or abstraction. The relation of the Church to the nation, therefore, is understood theologically only if the nation carries forward the function of the law in relation to the Gospel: Church is to nation as Gospel is to law. But that relation can be subverted in history by special interests, by indifference as well as by greed, and while in specific conflicts the relation seems to be fragile or expendable, it is worth fighting and perhaps dying for in the English context.

Niebuhr's understanding of the metaphoric relation of the Church to the nation was better understood, I suspect, in the nineteenth century than in the twentieth. Take, for example, Gladstone's message about the peculiar and enduring relation of the Church to the English nation. Gladstone argued that "the doctrine of the Church ... asserts the Divine origin and sanction of the power of governing" (Gladstone 1879, V: 243). In defining the national establishment of the Church of England, Gladstone wished to assert that in principle the relationship is legitimate regardless of the events which in his time were placing that relationship on trial. In principle the state is as important to the Church as it is to the family. The protections afforded the family by the state no more compromise the institution of the family than the protections afforded to the Church by the state necessarily compromise the Church. In the same way, then, the constraints provided by the state are for the protection of both institutions and do not *in principle* undermine their authority. As institutions, the family and the Church are of a divine order and in history precede the institution of the state that guarantees their historical continuity and responsible functioning. In denying the legitimacy of an establishment of the Church, Gladstone argues, the Church in the English settlement did not in principle sacrifice its own autonomy, since ecclesiastical law was intended from the outset to be made and administered by ecclesiastical lawyers, and the settlement assumed the prior consent of the clergy and also of the laity (pp. 251–53). In connection with the Church, the monarch was a faithful communicant as well as governor, and the Crown acted for itself rather than, as in Gladstone's time, through a Parliament of mixed composition and dubious concerns in religious matters (p. 248). Gladstone is certain that:

> "the forefathers of the English nation, when thus put upon their trial, will come honourably and well, due allowances being made, out of whatever scrutiny their conduct may be called to bear."
>
> (Gladstone 1879, V: 176)

Nations and civilizations are worth living and dying for, and their contributions to the Church are no less enduring and vital than the contribution made by the old Israel, living under the law, to the Church living under the Gospel and sovereignty of Christ. That relationship endures wherever the Church seeks to fulfill its own obedience to the divine principle of governance in history.

What that obedience requires of the Church depends, of course, on specific circumstances. Gladstone argues that the Church in the nineteenth century need not despise the work of its forefathers in establishing religion in order to be faithful to its changed circumstances. Part of the change is due to the Church's greed and laziness in accepting imaginary privileges from the state and in filling its own offices with unworthy and worldly officials (pp. 251–52). Part of these circumstances were due to the Church's new vitality after a century of silence and apathy when, during the 1700s, its convocations had been suppressed, its liturgies cold and inadequately attended. But the Church faced in Gladstone's times a situation very different from the circumstances of the initial establishment.

What had time done to make ancient good so uncouth? The ability of the Church to stand as a metaphor for the nation depends on the continued synthesis as well as tension between law and Gospel, state and Church, within the framework of the nation-state. But Gladstone mentions one factor in particular that makes the synthesis difficult and the tension potentially destructive of the social fabric: the heterogeneous social and religious character of the population and of its representation in a Parliament of "mixed belief" (p. 248), whose:

> "composition has rendered it progressively less fit to exercise even the qualified functions it has before possessed. Divisions of opinion have multiplied; the nation is broken up into many sects and religions; all claim the equal exercise of political power, and nearly every claim has been admitted."
>
> (Gladstone 1879, V: 262)

When the nation is divided in religious and sectarian loyalties, the state as such cannot provide a consistent framework but only a "bastard and deceptive consistency" (VI, p. 6) It would therefore be inauthentic for the state to profess a religious commitment that it patently lacks, and it would be destructive for such a state to exercise authority in the affairs of the Church.

Under these conditions, liturgical change is inevitably both political and divisive. Matters of ceremony rightly involve matters of doctrine, as Sykes has reminded us, no less in the present than during the tractarian reforms of the nineteenth century. But whereas the Church of England now has the legal autonomy to authorize alternative services, in Gladstone's era the authority of Parliament was necessary whether to resist or to institutionalize liturgical reforms. Gladstone therefore argued for *greater autonomy for the Church within the framework of the establishment* at least a century before that autonomy was granted. He warned that a controversial change in the *Book of Common Prayer* might otherwise produce the destruction of the establishment:

> "The Church ... is in near peril of the forfeiture of her solemn trust, and that the providence of God, which has hitherto so wonderfully kept her, makes now the most urgent calls upon the courage and sagacity of all who, whether as rulers or subjects, and

whether in the State or in the Church, have an interest and a share in the determination of her destinies."

(Gladstone 1879, V: 177)

This Niebuhrian warning reminds the Church that it works out its salvation only within history and therefore in fear and trembling. It has no other choice than to retain its purity by once again becoming a wanderer in exile from historical communities and nations if it fails to maintain its spiritual freedom within the framework of the establishment (p. 257).

Gladstone's warning suggests that liturgical controversies inevitably foreshadow a change in the relation between the Church and any national society. In England, of course, the controversies of the Church over matters of ritual had profound political consequences because the fact of establishment guaranteed that ecclesiastical quarrels would become national conflicts at the highest level. Gladstone gave his warning when the Church was fighting over whether priests should stand with their backs or their right sides toward the congregation while celebrating the Eucharist, while letters to the editor and parliamentary speeches carried the quarrel to the center of the nation and the state. He feared the controversy might end the establishment once and for all. But the Church's worship always defines the Church's place within the nation. Changes in the liturgy therefore announce a change in the relationship of the Church to its national context. Indeed, the content of the liturgy spells out the terms of that new relation. There is more than one kind of establishment for religion, and others besides the English have found a way to disestablish religion in their own time and country through changing their forms of worship.

The liturgical clues to a change in the Church's relation to the nation may be quite unsubtle. Since 1662 the English had been praying:

> "We beseech thee also to save and defend all Christian Kings, Princes, and Governors, and especially thy servant ELIZABETH our Queen, that under her we may be Godly and quietly governed: and grant unto her whole Council, and to all that are put in Authority under her that they may truly and indifferently minister Justice, to the punishment of wickedness, and vice, and to the maintenance of thy true religion and Virtue."

No doubt here that the ruler is a Christian charged with the responsibility of helping Christianity to flourish within the borders of the kingdom. When praying "for the Church," the congregation prays for the nation as though for itself by another name. But in 1928 the English revised this ancient prayer by saying:

> "We beseech thee also to lead all nations in the way of righteousness and peace; and so to direct all kings and rulers, that under them thy people may be godly and quietly governed. And grant unto thy servant ELIZABETH our Queen, and to all that are put in authority under her, that they may truly and impartially minister justice, to the punishment of wickedness and vice, and to the maintenance of thy true religion and virtue."

It is still not too much to hope for that the people of God will be governed in a godly and quiet manner, but the hope embraces all nations and not only those under Christian rulers: not a strange development as the Commonwealth comes to include Christian societies like Ireland within the same framework as nations governed by Muslims or others who worship merely tribal deities. But in expanding to a cosmopolitan framework the prayer contracts the scope of the Queen's religious identity; she is no long a "Christian" ruler, although she is charged with maintaining true religion and virtue. The monarchy has lost Christian substance if not Christian function by finding its place among the rulers of "all nations." A truly universal Church does not ask for a merely national homeland in which to realize its true nature. As hopes for a universal Christian community expand, the hope for a Christian society seems to contract.

Hope for a nation that like the Church is a confessing Christian community is absent from the pages of one recent revision (known as Series 2) in the Church of England. Whereas the prayer for the Church had previously included both the nation and the Church, the revision (Series 2) simply calls all these prayers "intercessions" and allows the clergy to pick and choose among various options; prayers for the Church being one, prayers for the nation being another.

The faithful pray "for the whole Church of God in Christ Jesus, and for all men according to their needs." This invitation leaves open the question of what is meant by the whole Church of God in Christ Jesus, but the text of the prayer itself mentions the Church explicitly only in the first set of instructions and petitions. The clergyman is told that:

> "he *may* pray for the Church throughout the world, and especially for the diocese and its Bishop; for any particular need of the

Church; and a short period of silence may be kept; after which he *may* say,

Lord, in thy mercy
Hear our prayer.
Grant that we who confess thy Name may be united in thy truth, live together in thy love, and show forth thy glory in the world [emphasis added]."

The clergyman is clearly not required to pray for the Church in these intercessions. The intercessions have other objects at times perhaps more pressing than the Church of England: a whole world, in fact, waiting for the showing forth of God's glory.

The distinction between the Church and the nation is pronounced at the outset and continues with the next instruction and petition for various countries and occupations:

"Here he *may* pray for the nations of the world, and especially for his kingdom and Elizabeth its Queen; for all men in their various callings; and again a short period of silence may be kept; after which he *may* say,

Lord, in thy mercy
Hear our prayer.
Direct this nation and all the nations in the ways of justice and of peace, that we may honour all men, and seek the common good [emphasis added]."

The Church is clearly no longer a metaphor for the Christian nation. One prays for England only in the same terms that one would pray for Pakistan or Iran, that they should follow the paths that lead to justice and peace and, by conferring honour on each person, find a common virtue in their national life. Even if the Church is still a city set upon a hill to remind all nations of their common origin and destiny, every nation can nevertheless fulfill its destiny without becoming Christian. Abstractions rather than proper names will do very nicely, if they are abstractions on the level of justice and peace.

Clearly there has been a profound change in the liturgical expression of what the Church hopes and prays for at the level of the nation. Even the Queen is rendered in the third person: "this kingdom and its Queen." Her vocation is not singularly Christian but simply to seek justice and the common good. She was once liturgically "our Queen," and the first person plural signified that the Queen is the head of a Church: a personification of the Church as a metaphor for the nation. Now the Queen and the English kingdom are both in the third person singular, where they are safely removed from any sacramental or official place within the Kingdom of God on earth.

The point is simply that the Church has clearly lowered its hopes for the nation *per se* as a legitimate manifestation of the Christian community. The Church now refers to the Queen as a liturgical option, and the option places the nation as one among the many nations of the world. Of course, that same Church recognizes the Queen as its highest officer and is addressed by the Queen herself in the first person plural. When speaking to the two synods of the Church of England convened during the last decade, the Queen unfailingly referred to herself and the Church as "we." Where "we" is used to speak both for the monarch and the Church itself, a liturgy that insists on separating its prayers for the nation and "its" ruler can only cast a discordant note. Gladstone, of course, warned that liturgical changes, if they are sensitive and contentious enough, may yet effect the disestablishment of religion at the national level.

The union of the English-speaking peoples has always been a precarious achievement: a marvel for which Cromwell gave the entire credit to the mighty acts of God whose servants skillfully employed an excellent combination of cavalry, footmen, and cannon on His behalf. Some individuals were disappointed in God's achievements, as Cromwell was sorry to note. But God has always had His detractors, just as the union of the English, Welsh, Scottish, and Irish has never been entirely secure. Populist loyalties to a class, a region, or a way of life threatened then, and still threaten, to break up the United Kingdom into parties and autonomous regions.

When individuals and groups express their loyalties through religion their civil differences are not only sublimated but raised to a higher power – intensified while literally being offered to God in enthusiastic prayer or solemn liturgy. As Gladstone observed during the heat of the liturgical reforms of the nineteenth century, matters of ceremony then become doctrinal issues that, under the terms of the national establishment of religion, in turn become civil disputes. The journey from lay loyalties to civil disturbance in the streets and in the courts has been traveled since the days of the pilgrimages in England, pilgrimages to the shrines of populist heroes who defied the monarchy. In the past the framework provided by religion to the emerging nation has been sufficiently elastic to encompass a landscape that colors regional or class loyalties with the intense hues of religious devotion and ideology. But it is no wonder that statesmen before and after Gladstone have feared that ceremony, in taking on doctrinal and civil significance, can yet disrupt the framework of an emerging nation.

What is required of ceremony, then, if it is to offer up these passionate loyalties without intensifying them into "sinful and inordinate affections"? I have already considered part of the answer to this question in pointing to the gap in the new liturgy between the prayers for the Church and the prayers for the nation. The gap frees local energies and commitments from a national framework and places the nation on the same footing with other nations in a secular twilight in which all national differences are rather gray. Only a ceremony that expresses and modifies the commitments of individuals and groups to their own kin, to their own place and people, to their co-workers and fellow sufferers, will make it possible for the laity to acknowledge that their affections and commitments may lack justice and spring from motives other than love itself. So long as these loyalties are to be offered and yet contained within a social framework as intense and limited as the nation, these loyalties will require cleansing as well as expression in the context of the liturgy. Take away the religious significance of the nation, and the nation itself will no longer act as a framework to receive and yet contain these energies and commitments. Pressures may still build up from within the nation, but they will be more volatile and will dissipate more readily through the gaps in the national framework. Such a dissipation of loyalty is not surprising when workers in textile mills find their counterparts or enemies in the mills of the Third World or when individuals petition a court in Strasbourg rather than in Parliament for final redress of certain grievances. The nation then becomes a veil, gauzy and easily removed, between local industrial valleys and international markets or competitors. If the liturgy simply reflects these changing circumstances rather than proclaims the Christian community's hope for a redeemed and witnessing national community, the task of achieving ecclesiastical unity is considerably simplified. Christians are free to proclaim their unity in the spirit and to pursue ecclesiastical reunion without let or hindrance by populist loyalties and national institutions. But the task of achieving unity within and between actual nations becomes immeasurably more difficult.

The new rites provide a liturgy for a mass society rather than for the new nation emerging from the conflicts and sacrifices of the people of God. Individuals who have lost a basic function in creating their society are given ceremonial functions. The reality of corporate action is replaced by the image of participation, carefully contrived as in the "wired" political conventions of American parties to allow a wide range of individuals to make their appearances. The laity appear in one role or another like the transient figures on a convention's podium. When asked for their deepest personal experiences they are given rather bland lines to utter in order to avoid disruptive and highly subjective emotional states. It is not surprising that the ecstatic and charismatic religious movements of the past two decades have coincided with the emergence of these rationalized texts in which the heights and depths of personal and corporate experience are leveled and made plain. It is also wholly understandable that so many individuals in search of the symbols and symbolic actions by which they can tap their most intense motivations and sacrifice themselves for the highest good have found these symbols outside the Church during these decades of rationally administered liturgical change.

If the laity know that their highest aspirations for equality among all people are tainted with a drive for power and domination, they will offer their souls and bodies only in the context of the most profound penitence. Otherwise, in the drive to construct a new society on the grounds of equality and brotherhood, they will not fail, as Eliot once warned us, "to ignore some essential aspect of reality"; the price of that ignorance, he noted, is the "ultimate destruction of the new nation" (Eliot [1940], 1949: 50). On one side of the Atlantic we have Eliot warning that even a wholly Christian society will need "constant reform" because it relies on individuals whose motives are "primarily worldly and selfish" (p. 47). But in a Christian society the law and the ordering of society is "a schoolmaster to bring us to Christ," a point William Temple insisted upon in calling England to its destiny to be a Christian nation. The nation will emerge as a coherent and egalitarian community, in which domination is limited, open to criticism and continual reform, only if the Church indeed remains a metaphor for what the nation is at heart, is in its calling and will be at the end. Otherwise the law and the social order are simply imposed to contain the selfishness and egoism in all institutions and in all strivings for greater equality without hope of future transformation. On the American side of the Atlantic it is Niebuhr's voice that sounds the same note:

"the community is the frustration as well as the realization of individual life. Its collective egotism is an offense to his conscience; its institutional injustices negate the ideal of justice; and such brotherhood as it achieves is limited by ethnic and geographic boundaries."

(Niebuhr 1953: 11, 310)

Only a community that knows itself unworthy to offer any sacrifice can be trusted with the task of foreshadowing the structure and boundaries of the emergent nation. Otherwise the Church becomes, not a metaphor for the possibilities of community and equality within the nation, but a reflection of the institutional injustice, the domination of ordinary people by élites, and the collective egoism of the larger society.

Ironically, perhaps, even as it appears that the Church has lost its power to transform the nation or the nation its capacity partially to fulfill the Church's mission in history, strong calls are being made to repentance and obedience on the national scale. In the United States, as I have noted, religion has renewed its political drive. Catholics are being summoned by their bishops to political judgments, while Catholic politicians are calling for a judicious suspension of religious judgments in political contexts. Dismissed by commentators as authoritarian and dogmatic, fundamentalists and evangelical Christians are calling for Christians to remember and exercise their commitments to the family and the nation as they vote for various candidates. Not as likely as some intellectuals to pour contempt on their national pride, evangelical Christians are also more likely than those they dub "secular humanists" to call for national repentance. The notion that nations will answer on the Day of Judgment has survived biblical criticism, and evangelicals in England as well as in the United States are calling for Christians to respect the nation as a fact of history under the providence of God. Neither condemn the nation as unworthy of being a vehicle for divine grace nor make the nation the final stage of the Christian's pilgrimage on earth. The nation and the Church are two communities whose historical destinies are inseparable yet wholly distinguished from one another.

Conclusion

Rituals in relatively simple societies provided a powerful but limited release of energy and passion that might otherwise have torn apart a community and threatened those in positions of authority. Durkheim observed that annual orgies not only released passions but reinforced tribal limits by temporarily suspending them (Durkheim [1915], 1965: 236). Girard has argued that rituals give symbolic expression and release to destructive emotions that might once again erupt into collective violence unless remembered, recalled, released, and controlled through collective ritual (Girard 1977:19). Burkert argues that the primitive fears and satisfactions of the hunt, and later, of the slaying of animals find expression and a safe limit in ancient Greek rituals of sacrifice (Burkert 1979: 54). But there is no guarantee that ritual can serve these functions in modern societies. Indeed, Lasch is arguing that even modern sports cannot contain the competitive and aggressive strivings of their participants or spectators (Lasch 1979). The question is whether *any* ritual can now provide the cathartic and symbolic expression of destructive emotions that threaten to erupt through the surface of social life.

The nature of the emotional bond forged by ritual will depend, of course, on the kind of society and the kind of people within it. Until fairly recently, studies of ritual have focused on communities or tribes that are "highly structured, cyclical, and repetitive" (Turner 1969: 188). Because they are so highly structured, virtually every person holds a position, and in times of ritual celebration the authority of virtually every position will be attacked or defended. Because they are cyclical, limits that are suspended will be restored. Rituals that are "liminal" will allow servants to harass their masters, tenants to throw mud at their landlords, debtors to revile their creditors, and the poor to strut like the rich (Turner 1969: 166 ff.). But because these societies are cyclical, every gesture of defiance leads to a return of deference, and the poor once again show respect, if only for a time, to the rich. The cyclical nature of the society suggests that the change of seasons is an appropriate time to let loose the suppressed spirits in the community. Turner aptly describes Halloween in this connection:

"Halloween, in Western culture, with its emphases on the powers of children and earth spirits, precedes two traditional Christian feasts that represent structural levels of Christian cosmology – i.e., All Saints' and All Souls' . . . All Souls' Day . . . commemorates the souls in purgatory, emphasizing at once their lower hierarchical position to the souls in heaven, and the active communitas of the living, who ask the saints to intercede for those undergoing liminal ordeal in purgatory and the saved dead both in heaven and in purgatory."

(Turner 1969: 181–82)

In modern societies, however, traditional rituals will not easily give such satisfaction to an entire population. No less structured than more primitive societies, modern nations lack a single hierarchy of authority and prestige; on the contrary, few grievances against persons in authority are shared by an entire population. Even the memorial to the veterans of the Vietnam War provides only a controversial focal point for those members of the population with strong feelings about the war. Many members of the population will not be addressed by that memorial, and those who do respond to it deeply will not be of one mind. It is a fitting monument, perhaps, to an undeclared war that cannot therefore be finished. The actions of that war remain unconsummated, whether as acts of national courage or national shame. Rather than have a cyclical recurrence of that war or of martial seasons, the nation experiences intermittent and protracted periods of partial mobilization for a variety of threats. New situations like current hostilities in Central America raise fears and hatreds associated with the Vietnam War, but these unfinished animosities, precisely because they remain unfinished, can only color and distort rather than adequately shape national responses to the new threats. As wars are neither declared nor finished, so also has peace become a mere process rather than an act in which a new world is declared and an old battle finished once and for all.

In these chapters I have argued that secularization has made it less possible for the sacred to correct, to complete, and to fulfill action. The restriction of the sacred to separate spheres of competence, a professionalized clergy, a bureaucratic Church, a laity claiming increased measures of influence and respect, and the proliferation of options, make sacred authority itself more abstract, more optional, and more utilitarian: an achievement, however limited, rather than a gift. It may also be true that secularization makes it somewhat less necessary for social systems to have adequate rituals for completing and fulfilling actions. The institutionalization of the notion of a lifetime of continuous testing, the separation of personal from official capacities in secular roles, and the widespread ethic of rational responsibility make secular authority reasonably reliable and autonomous.

Nonetheless, a life of continuous testing and trial is often exhausting for the incumbents of any roles. In a democratic society many are called and tested continuously for such responsibility. Virtually no one is simply chosen. Again, the failings of all in authority generate misgivings and cause grievances that must eventually be satisfied. Demands for a public accounting, even for a final, historical judgment intensify the need for rituals that can satisfy such grievances, complete what is missing in any incumbent's qualifications for social authority, and pass judgment on their failings. In times of trial, these pressures enter politics and even the streets.

No society can survive with ease or confidence when its members do not trust one another or respect their leaders. It is a truism, of course, that legitimate authority is essential to the survival of any community or nation, and social scientists still monitor the steady erosion of the American public's trust in the President or in major institutions like the Supreme Court, the Church, and big business. At the heart of this truism, however, is a somewhat more poignant truth: that humans hunger for reality in each other's words and deeds. Sham, the feigning of affection or respect, corrodes the most essential ties of trust, whether in the family or in the nation-state. We scrutinize our leaders for signs of fakery, and we do so with good reason. The body politic loses heart when its leaders cannot be trusted, just as certainly as when children cannot believe their parents or parishioners cannot have faith in their priest. Without such authenticity, a people will demand a day in court when their grievances can be heard and their demands satisfied.

Pressures for such a day of judgment are rapidly mounting in Western societies. Several countries reveal a chronic distrust of authority and an equally chronic suspicion of public appearances. The narratives of Watergate are enough to tell the more recent American episodes in this story, although the erosion of public trust has been documented for many years prior to the Nixon administration and continues unabated (Lipset and Schneider 1982). Part of the erosion, of course, is also due to the roles themselves; they seem to require only partial and temporary transformations in modern societies. In speaking of the revolution of 1848, Carlyle wrote of the sudden awareness that rules of obligation were illusory; the Sicilians thus repudiated any obligations to Italy and Naples and the French denied obligations to the King. The realization that those in power are simply individuals playing the role of the King leads to the discovery that the emperor has no clothes. The separation of the person from the office denudes the office of personal obligations and the person of official authority.

To discover that the King is merely playing a part, and to discover that the King agrees that he has been merely play-acting, is to undermine the rituals of obligation and release. What ritual can undo the damage described in this passage by Carlyle?

> "Democracy, on this new occasion, finds all Kings *conscious* that they are but play actors. The miserable mortals, enacting their High Life Below Stairs, with faith only that this Universe may be all a phantasm and hypocrisis, – the truculent Constable of the Destinies suddenly enters: 'Scandalous Phantasms,' what do you here? Are 'solemnly constituted imposters' the proper Kings of men? ... Ye miserable, this Universe is not an upholstery Puppet-play but a terrible God's Fact and you, I think – had you not better be gone!"
>
> (Carlyle 1969: 6)

Carlyle attributes the Sicilian revolt, and later the Parisian rebellion, to the effect of the Pope who claimed to take the New Testament as his only guide and who initiated a climate of reform within the Church. Like the present Pope, whose visit to Poland rekindled nationalist dreams and emboldened the working class to demand autonomous unions, the Pope of 1848 displayed a revolutionary authenticity in the fusion of person and role. In juxtaposition to papal authenticity, the European kings appeared, as Carlyle put it, to be sham indeed. The religious dream does not die, even when ritual fails to support it and the nation itself gives the dream little foothold in reality. It can be ignored, this dream, only at some peril. That is why, given the present complexity of the nation-state and of modern rites, I would argue that the dream itself be given more consideration, even though that may mean a call to reduce or dismantle the state itself.

In the old Israel the myth of the covenant and of the Messianic king created obligations that bound the worshipper as citizen to the Kingdom of God rather than to the nation's king. As David Martin argued, religious language, enacted and acted upon in ritual, creates the *double entendre* of words such as "king" and "prince" (Martin 1978b: 1). It is impossible to have "no king but Caesar" when one has another king who stands as the prototype of all legitimate rule.

Next to that kingship, as Carlyle pointed out, the kingdoms of this world run the danger of appearing to be sham. As the New Testament put it, the anointing of the Christian ruler unmasks the principalities and powers of this age.

Even in modern societies, sacred authority may still create a demand for ultimate judgment that unsettles secularized political authority. Iran seeks to put the United States on trial, just as the Catholic Left sought in the American courts to place the Vietnam War and the American government on trial. The demand for a trial to end all trials underlies the resurgence of millennial religion in the West as well as in the East. Millions in the United States alone listen to broadcasts promising an imminent last judgment that will bring a verdict on the enemies of God and rapture for His friends. While millions appear actively to believe in and await such a final judicial review of our historical proceedings, millions more have initiated a quasi-judicial review of American politicians and policies in the name of the highest authority. For some the Eschaton is too late in coming, for others it is imminent. For both, "now" is always the time to purify the body politic: to put the national house in order or to take it down.

References

Allcock, J. B. (ed.) (1982) *Pragmatism and Sociology*. Cambridge: Cambridge University Press.

Almond, G. A. and Verba, S. (1963) *The Civil Culture*. Princeton, NJ: Princeton University Press.

Archer, M. and Vaughan, M. (1970) Education, Secularization, Desecularization, and Resecularization. In D. A. Martin and M. Hill (eds) *A Sociological Yearbook of Religion in Britain* 3. London: SCM Press.

Arendt, H. (1978) *The Life of the Mind*. New York: Harcourt Brace Jovanovich.

Austin, J. L. (1982) *How to Do Things With Words*. Oxford: Oxford University Press.

Becker, E. (1975) *Escape From Evil*. New York: Free Press.

Bell, D. (1976) *The Cultural Contradictions of Capitalism*. New York: Basic Books.

Bellah, R. N. (1980) Religion and Legitimation in the American Republic. In Thomas Robbins and Richard Anthony (eds) *In God We Trust*. New Brunswick, NJ: Transaction Books.

——, Madsden, R., Sullivan, W. M., Swidler, A., and Tipton, S. M. (1985) *Habits of the Heart: Individualism and Commitment in American Life*. Berkeley, CA: University of California Press.

Berger, P. L. (1963) *Invitation to Sociology: A Humanistic Perspective*. Garden City, New York: Anchor Books.

Bernstein, B. (1974) *Class, Codes and Control, Vol. 1: Theoretical Studies Towards a Sociology of Language*. London: Routledge & Kegan Paul.

——, (1975) *Class, Codes and Control, Vol. 3: Towards a Theory of Educational Transmissions*. London: Routledge & Kegan Paul.

Bloch, M. (ed.) (1975) *Political Language and Oratory in Traditional Society*. London and New York: Academic Press.

168 · The Dream of the Perfect Act

Bocock, R. (1974) *Ritual in Industrial Society: A Sociological Analysis of Ritualism in Modern England*. London: Allen & Unwin.
Boyer, R. E. (ed.) (1966) *Oliver Cromwell and the Puritan Revolt: Failure of a Man or a Faith?* Boston: D. C. Heath.
Brook, S. (1965) *The Language of the Book of Common Prayer*. New York: Oxford University Press.
Buchanan, C. O. (ed.) (1968) *Modern Anglican Liturgies, 1958–1968*. London and New York: Oxford University Press.
Burkert, W. (1979) *Structure and History in Greek Mythology*. Berkeley, CA: University of California Press.
Carlyle, Thomas (1969) *A Carlyle Reader: Selections from the Writings of Thomas Carlyle*. Edited by G. B. Tennyson. New York: Modern Library.
Carroll, J. (1977) *Puritan, Paranoid, Remissive: A Sociology of Modern Culture*. London, Henley and Boston: Routledge & Kegan Paul.
——, (1981) The Role of Guilt in the Formation of Modern Society: England 1359–1800. *British Journal of Sociology* 32 (4): 459–503.
Chadwick, O. (1975) *The Secularization of the European Mind in the Nineteenth Century: The Gifford Lectures in the University of Edinburgh for 1973–1974*. Cambridge: Cambridge University Press.
Chauncy, C. (1742) Enthusiasm Described and Cautioned Against. In D. B. Rutnam (ed.) *The Great Awakening: Event and Exegesis*. New York: John Wiley, 1970.
Cromwell, Thomas (1846) *Letters and Speeches*. vols. with elucidations by Thomas Carlyle. London: Chapman and Long.
Dobbelaere, K. (1981) *Secularization: A Multi-Dimensional Concept*. Sage Publications for the International Sociological Association, *Current Sociology* 29 (2), Summer.
Döbert, R. (1973) Systemtheorie und die Entwicklung religioser Deutungsysteme: Zur Logic des sozialwissenschaften Funktionalismus. Frankfurt am Main, Suhrkamp Verlag.
Durkheim, E. (1915) *The Elementary Forms of the Religious Life: A Study in Religious Sociology*. Translated by J. W. Swain. London: Allen & Unwin, 1965.
——, (1938) *The Rules of Sociological Method*. 8th edn. Translated by S. A. Solovay and J. H. Mueller, edited by G. E. G. Catlin. Glencoe, IL: Free Press.
——, (1955) *Pragmatism and Sociology*. Translated by J. C. Whitehouse; edited and introduced by J. B. Allcock. Cambridge: Cambridge University Press, 1982.
Edelson, M. (1976) Toward a Study of Interpretation in Psychoanalysis. In J. Loubser, R. C. Baum, A. Effret, and V. M. Lidz (eds) *Explorations in General Theory in Social Science*, vol. I. New York: Free Press.
Eliot, T. (1930) *The Complete Poems and Plays 1909–1950*. New York: Harcourt, Brace.
——, (1940) *Christianity and Culture: The Idea of a Christian Society and Notes Toward the Definition of Culture*. New York: Harcourt, Brace, and World, 1949.

Erikson, E. (1959) Identity and the Life Cycle. Monograph. *Psychological Issues* 1 (1). New York: International Universities Press.

——, (1968) *Identity, Youth and Crisis*. New York: W. W. Norton.

——, (1977) *Toys and Reasons: Stages in the Ritualization of Experience*. New York: W. W. Norton.

——, (ed.) (1978) *Adulthood*. New York: W. W. Norton.

Etzioni, A. (1982) *Immodest Agenda: Rebuilding America Before the Twenty First Century*. New York: McGraw-Hill.

Fanon, F. (1967) *Black Skins, White Masks*. New York: Grove Press.

Fenn, R. K. (1982) *Liturgies and Trials. The Secularization of Religious Language*. Oxford: Blackwell.

Firth, C. H. (1938) *Oliver Cromwell and the Rule of the Puritans in England*. London: Oxford University Press. Quoted in R. E. Boyer, *Oliver Cromwell and the Puritan Revolt*. Boston: D. C. Heath, 1966

Fromm, E. (1957) *The Forgotten Language: An Invitation to the Understanding of Dreams, Fairytales and Myths*. New York: Rinehart & Winston.

Gaustad, Edwin S. L. (1954) A Great and General Awakening. In D. B. Rutman (ed.) *The Great Awakening: Event and Exegesis*. New York: John Wiley, 1970

Gerth, H. H. and Mills, C. W. (1958) *From Max Weber: Essays in Sociology*. New York: Oxford University Press.

Girard, R. (1977) *Violence and the Sacred*. Baltimore, MD: Johns Hopkins University Press.

Gladstone, W. E. (1879) *Gleanings of Past Years, 1843–78*. New York: Charles Scribner's Sons, vols V–VI.

Gluckman, M. (1965) *Politics, Law, and Ritual in Tribal Society*. Chicago: Aldine.

Goffman, E. (1981) *Forms of Talk*. Philadelphia: University of Pennsylvania Press.

Habermas, J. (1975) *Legitimation Crisis*. Translated by T. McCarthy. Boston: Beacon Press.

Halliday, M. (1978) *Language as Social Semiotic: The Social Interpretation of Language and Meaning*. London: Edward Arnold.

Harrison, J. (1962) *Epilegomena to the Study of Greek Religion and Themis: The Study of the Social Origins of Greek Religion*. New Hyde Park, New York: University Books.

Heimert, A. (1966) Toward the Republic. In D. B. Rutman (ed.) *The Great Awakening: Event and Exegesis*. New York: John Wiley, 1970.

Herberg, W. (1967) Religion in a Secularized Society: The New Shape of Religion in America. In R. D. Knudten (ed.) *The Sociology of Religion; An Anthology*. New York: Appleton-Century-Crofts.

Holmes, U. T. (1981) Education for Liturgy. In M. C. Burson (ed.) *Worship Points the Way*. New York: Seabury Press.

Homan, R. (1981) Sociology and the Questionable Truth. In D. Martin and P. Mullen (eds) *No Alternative*. Oxford, England: Basil Blackwell.

Kelly, A. (1950) *Eleanor of Aquitaine and the Four Kings*. Cambridge, MA: Harvard University Press.

Kolakowski, L. (1982) *Religion*. Fontana Paperbacks.

Kozol, J. (1975) *The Night Is Dark*. New York: Continuum, 1980.

Ladner, G. B. (1967) *The Idea of Reform, Its Impact on Christ: Thought and Action in the Age of the Fathers*. New York: Harper & Row.

Lane, C. (1981) *The Rites of Rulers, Ritual in Industrial Society: The Soviet Case*. Cambridge, England, and New York: Cambridge University Press.

Lasch, C. (1979) *The Culture of Narcissism*. New York: W. W. Norton; Warner Books 1980.

Levinson, D. J., Darrow, C. N., Klein, G. B, Levinson, M. H. and McKee, B. (1978) *Seasons of a Man's Life*. New York: Holt Rinehart & Winston.

Lifton, R. J. (1967) *Boundaries: Psychological Man in Revolution*. New York: Simon & Schuster, 1969.

——, (1973) *Home from the War, Vietnam Veterans: Neither Victims nor Executioners*. New York: Simon & Schuster.

——, (1976) *The Life of the Self: Toward a New Psychology*. New York: Harper & Row.

Lipset, S. M. and Schneider, W. (1982) *The Confidence Gap: Business, Labor, and Government in The Public Mind*. New York: Free Press.

Loevinger, J. (1976) *Ego Development: Concepts and Theories* (with A. Blasi). San Francisco: Jossey Bass.

Luckmann, T. (1967) *The Invisible Religion: The Problem of Religion in Modern Society*. New York: Macmillan.

Malinowski, B. (1948) *Magic, Science and Religion* and other essays: Selected, and with an introduction by R. Redfield. Boston: Beacon Press.

Martin, D. (1978a) *A General Theory of Secularization*. Oxford, England: Basil Blackwell.

——, (1978b) *The Dilemmas of Contemporary Religion*. Oxford, England: Basil Blackwell.

——, (1980) *The Breaking of the Image: A Sociology of Christian Theory and Practice*. Oxford, England: Basil Blackwell.

Martin, B. (1983) The Christian Ethic and the Spirit of Security and Deterrence. In D. Martin and P. Mullen (eds) *Unholy Warfare: The Church and the Bomb*. Oxford, England: Basil Blackwell.

——, (1983) Invisible Religion, Popular Culture, and Anti-Nuclear Sentiment. In D. Martin and P. Mullen (eds) *Unholy Warfare: The Church and the Bomb*. Oxford, England: Basil Blackwell.

Mayhew, L. (ed.) (1982) *Talcott Parsons on Institutions and Social Evolution*. Chicago: University of Chicago Press.

Merton, R. L. (1957) *Social Theory and Social Structure*. Rev. and enl. edn. London: Collier-Macmillan.

Mills, C. W. (1966) *Sociology and Pragmatism*. New York: Oxford University Press.

Mitscherlich, A. (1970) *Society Without the Father: A Contribution to Social Psychology*. New York: Schocken Books.

Moore, S. F. (1977) Political Meetings and the Simulation of Unanimity: Kilimanjaro. In S. F. Moore and B. G. Meyerhoff (eds) *Secular Ritual*. Assen: Van Corcum.

Morris, B. (ed.) (1980) *Ritual Murder: Essays on Liturgical Reform*. Manchester: Carcanet Press.

News of Liturgy (1975) 3:2. Nottingham, England.

Niebuhr, R. (1935) *An Interpretation of Christian Ethics*. New York and London: Harper.

——, (1949) *Faith and History: A Comparison of Christian and Modern Views of History*. New York: Charles Scribner's Sons.

——, (1952) *The Irony of American History*. New York: Charles Scribner's Sons.

——, (1953) *The Nature and Destiny of Man*. 2 vols. New York: Charles Scribner's Sons.

Nisbet, R. (1969) *Social Change and History: Aspects of the Western Theory of Development*. New York: Oxford University Press.

O'Keefe, D. L. (1982) *Stolen Lightning: The Social Theory of Magic*. New York: Vintage Books, 1983.

O'Neill, J. P. (1972) *Sociology as a Skin Trade: Essays Towards a Reflexive Sociology*. New York: Harper Torchbooks.

——, (1976) The Hobbesian Problem in Marx and Parsons. In J. Loubser, R. C. Baum, A. Effrat, and V. M. Lidz (eds) *Explorations in General Theory in Social Science*, vol. I, ch. 12. New York: Free Press.

Parabola (1981) VI, 3:3.

Parsons, T. (1949) *Essays in Sociological Theory Pure and Applied*. Glencoe, Ill: The Free Press.

Quinney, R. (1980) *Providence: The Reconstruction of Social and Moral Order*. New York and London: Longman.

Robinson, J. A. T. (1950) *In the End, God: A Study of the Christian Doctrine of the Last Things*. London: James Clarke.

——, (1957) *Jesus and His Coming*. London: SCM Press.

Rubenstein, R. (1975) *The Cunning of History*. New York: Harper & Row.

Rutman, D. B. (ed.) (1970) *The Great Awakening: Event and Exegesis*. New York: John Wiley.

Sennett, R. (1980) *Authority*. New York: A. Knopf.

—— and Cobb, J. (1966) *The Hidden Injuries of Class*. New York: Vintage Books, 1973.

Shapiro, M. (1981) *Courts: A Comparative and Political Analysis*. Chicago: University of Chicago Press.

Shils, E. (1972) *The Intellectuals and the Powers and Other Essays*. Chicago: University of Chicago Press.

Silverman, D. and Torode, B. (1980) *The Material Word: Some Theories of Language and Its Limits*. London: Routledge & Kegan Paul.

Silverman, L. H., Lachmann, F. M., and Milich, R. H. (1982) *The Search for Oneness*. New York: International Universities Press.

Swanston, H. F. G. (1976) *A Language for Madness: The Abuse and Use of Christian Creeds*. Essex: Van Gorcum.

Sykes, S. W. (1978) *The Integrity of Anglicanism*. London and Oxford: Mowbray's.

Trickett, R. (1981) Cranmer not Irrelevant. In D. Martin and P. Mullen (eds) *No Alternative*. Oxford, England: Basil Blackwell.

Turner, V. (1969) *The Ritual Process: Structure and Anti-Structure*. Chicago: Aldine.

Underhill, E. (1937) *Worship*. New York and London: Harper.
Weinstein, F. and Platt, G. M. (1973) *Psychoanalytic Sociology: An Essay on the Interpretation of Historical Data and the Phenomena of Collective Behavior*. Baltimore, MD, and London: Johns Hopkins University Press.
West, C. C. (1967) Community – Christian and Secular. In H. Cox (ed.) *The Church Amid Revolution*. New York: Association Press.
——, (1978) Theology and Politics. (Unpublished mimeograph.)
Williams, H. A. (1964) Psychological objections. In D. M. MacKinnon, H. A. Williams, A. R. Vidler, and J. S. Bezzant, *Objections to Christian Belief*. Philadelphia and New York: J. B. Lippincott.
Wilson, B. (1956) *Magic and the Millennium*. Frogmore, Herts, England: Paladin, 1975.
——, (1975) *The Noble Savages: The Primitive Origins of Charisma and Its Contemporary Survival*. Berkeley, CA: University of California Press, a Quantum Book.
——, (1982) *Religion in Sociological Perspective*. New York: Oxford University Press.

Name Index

Subject Index

abstract values 42
act: notion of xvii–xix, 2–3; as social fact 1, 3–4, 16–18; *see also* actions; death of dream?; perfect act; thresholds
actions: acts reduced to 127; as acts 5, 17–18, 22, 26–31, 88–9; collective *see* society; motive and 7–8, 13; and response *see* third threshold
addressing: God 107; people 115–16; *see also under* discourse
adjudication *see* law
adulthood, transition to *see* initiation
aggressive motive 44–55
alienation 93–4, 120
All Souls' and All Saints' days 162
Alternative Service Book 43, 44, 68–70, 74
Anglicans *see* Church of England
anxiety 45; as impediment to crossing first threshold 35–7
asceticism 42
associations: limiting 82–5; membership of 26
atonement for guilt 93
authoritarian regime 128
authority: Church, secularized 75–8, 81–2; distrust of 164; individual 111–13, 117, 119, 120, 122, 129; of laity 150; organizational

75–6, 87, 114–16, 125; Puritans and 91, 93–5, 97; religious roles without 113–14

"bad faith" 62
baptism 37, 43, 45; discourse in 104; as maverick rite xi–xii; new rites ix, 68–9, 70, 79–81
being and wonder 85
Belgium 19
Bengali revolt 53
Berrigans (dissidents) 127
birth anxiety 35, 37
"blame" 94
Book of Common Prayer xvi, 74, 84, 130, 134, 136, 145, 149, 154
boundaries *see* public and private
Britain *see* England
bureaucracy 48; Church *see* Liturgical Commission

Calvinism 109, 122
capitalism 94–5, 120
Catholic Church 15, 19, 109
Catonsville Nine, trial of 128
center and periphery 121–22, 139
change and progress 7
charismatic individual 113
choice: plurality in education 57, 65, 67; *see also* multiplicity
Church: as metaphor for social life,

fourth threshold: binding individual and society in one act 16–17, 22–33; renewals of individual and society 28–33

fourth threshold: institutionalizing principle of will 118–41, 163; dualism 135–41; voluntarism institutionalized 121–24, 125–29; voluntarism, attempts to ritualize 129–35

France: monarchy, decline of 139, 164–65; power of church limited 121

freedom, institutionalized 20

Garden of Eden xx, 117

generations xi–xiii; collapse of differences between 50–2, 54–7, 87, 128–29; see also initiation

gifts, exchange of 64

God: addressing 107; law of 118, 146–47; on trial 117; people of see nation

"grace" 139

groups see associations

guilt: atonement for 93; expressed in confession 56; relieving burden of 20

Halloween 162

hatred see aggressive motive

heterogeneity of population 154

history and providence 6

hope, religious, in modern world see perfect act

hostility see aggressive motive

hunting xviii–xix, 162

id 38

ideal-typical act 6

identity crisis xii–xiii, 57–8

illness 49; as subjugation to fantasy 38

illusion 42

imperfect acts 12

implicit commands see indirect speech

Incarnation as act 3, 5–6

indirect speech 60–1, 68, 69–70

individual/personal: authority 107–17; 119, 120, 122, 129; charismatic 113; prototype 40–1; Puritans and 91, 93–4; rationality 22–33, 108–09; righteousness 43; ritual and 46; salvation 20, 92–4, 107, 109; social life as construction of 39; and society, bound see fourth threshold; and society, renewals of 28–33; truth and 4

initiation rites/rites of passage ix, x–xii, 43, 50–2, 87, 113, 115; lack of 126–27, 128; see also generations

institutionalization: of freedom 20; of voluntarism 121–24, 125–29

intelligibility and actions as acts 5

intention: motive and 7, 27, 119; see also first threshold

"intercessions," prayers as 156–57

Iran 143, 165

irrationality 24; see also rationality

irreversibility of acts 119

Israel, new 122–23, 143–44, 147

Jesus xi; contradiction in person and work of 120; see also crucifixion; Emmaus; Incarnation; Last Supper

Judeo-Christian tradition 123, 165

judgment see Last Judgment; law; trial

"juridical" habit 149–50

justice see law

kingship see monarchy

labeling theory 18

labor, alienation of 93–4

laity: roles of 113–14; see also people of God

language of worship 13–15; revised 65, 72–80, 82–4, 149

language, poetic 85

Last Judgment 144–47, 149, 161

Last Supper 11, 27, 60

law/justice/legislation 1, 6, 20, 160; discourse 110; dissatisfaction with 17; of God 118, 146–7; Gospel and 152; Liturgical Commission and 75–6

liberal regimes 127–28

Liturgical Commission of Church of England xv–xvii, 60–1, 71, 76, 131; deconsecration of church 75–6; language 65, 72–5, 77–80; see also baptism; marriage

liturgy, change in ix, xiv–xvii, 15, 66, 129–36; and death of dream 148–50, 154–55, 157–59; in USA xvi–xvii, 76, 134, 137; see also Liturgical Commission; worship

logic of social action, problem of 119–20

"made up" mind 37–8

marriage 82,86

martyrdom see self-sacrifice